You *Can*
If
You Think
You Can

The Power of Thinking
BIG

Electronic and soft cover print versions
Published by the Wellness Institute, Inc.,
1007 Whitney Ave., Gretna, LA 70056,
July 1, 2001

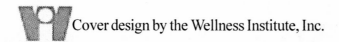 Cover design by the Wellness Institute, Inc.

SelfHelpBooks.com is a division of the
Wellness Institute, Inc.
Gretna, LA 70056

ISBN: 1-58741-083-4
Printed in the United States of America

You *Can* If You Think You Can

The Power of Thinking
BIG

Big Bill Rinaldi

Publisher's Foreword

After over 25 years of helping people cope with life's problems, one resounding truth has become absolutely clear to me - the importance of strong family/ social ties and a positive attitude. With these two crucial factors, people are unquestionably better able to cope with adversity. Those who lack a supportive network and do not think positively have a significantly harder time dealing with life's inevitable problems. Research consistently shows that those with a strong support network and a positive attitude tend to experience better mental and physical health than those who do not possess these two factors.

A remarkable individual, who at an early age experienced one of the greatest physical hardships imaginable - severe muscular dystrophy - has written the book you are about to read. Even though the severity of this serious disease would challenge the spirits of most of us, Bill Rinaldi approached this problem with an impressive degree of self-confidence and faith in himself.

Bill Rinaldi's story is a story of inspiration. It is a story of the incredible resiliency and strength of the human spirit. It is a story that needs to be shared with others.

When I first read Bill's story, I knew immediately that it was a story that would inspire others faced with similar adversity. I knew that people struggling with their own problems would find comfort and confidence from his story. I told Bill that we wanted to publish his book. I did, however, tell him that I had one suggestion. Even though Bill stands only 4' 11" tall, I asked him if I could add the appendage "Big" to his name. Because of the larger than life nature of his accomplishments, I felt that this addition to his name was fitting.

You Can If You Think You Can, explains how Big Bill Rinaldi not only dealt with adversity in a positive manner, but shows the reader that he is a person who has gone on to achieve accomplishments of which most of us could only wish.

Harold H. Dawley, Jr., Ph.D., ABPP
Publisher

Author's Preface

I feel so fortunate that I sometimes almost feel guilty. I am in the middle of my 55th year as I write this preface. I ask myself, as I have so many times before, how could anyone be as blessed as I have been. Being born into a loving, close- knit family, with understanding parents was my first blessing. Having many dear friends and inspiring, supportive teachers is another blessing. Finding my special person, my loving wife, was still another blessing. And being able to achieve more in life than anyone could ask for is still another blessing. Yes, the good Lord has indeed been kind to me.

Even though muscular dystrophy severely limited me physically from birth, this disease has not prevented me from living a full and contented life. I feel successful both personally and professionally. When reflecting on how life has been so good to me, one thought frequently comes to my mind. In addition to being surrounded by loving and caring people, I learned early on the importance of thinking positive. I learned that most of our failures comes from not trying. I discovered that if I put my mind to it and applied myself toward some goal or objective, more often than not, I was able to achieve it. Sure, I did not get everything I wanted, but I got enough.

Shakespeare said, "Life is made up of mingled yarn, some good and some bad." There is some good and some bad in all of our lives. The secret to succeeding in life is to focus on the good. It is my hope that this book in some simple way will help you know that - *You Can If You Think You Can.*

Bill Rinaldi

Dedication

To Mary, Mom, and Dad

and to those who believed I could

Table Of Contents

CHAPTER 1

Loving Parents and Strong Family Ties

In the summer of 1945, the first atomic bomb was dropped on Hiroshima. Shortly thereafter, another one was dropped on Nagasaki. A third explosion also occurred in Dunmore, the birth of a six-pound, eight-ounce dynamo, who just happens to be me.

On Sunday, July 8, 1945, in the waning twilight, a bouncing, blue-eyed, healthy baby boy was born. My arrival brought unbridled joy to my young parents, Alex and Rosebud Rinaldi. They welcomed their child as a healthy gift from God. Their soaring expectations knew no bounds as they looked forward to a bright and promising future. Little did they know the cruel surprises that fate had in store for them.

As mother held me, she and Alex prayed aloud, "God, bless our son with good health and happiness. Guide us to be good parents and let our boy grow to make us proud."

"God will hear our prayers," Alex said reassuringly.

"I have no doubt," she agreed.

Buoyed by their faith, my parents believed that their union had already met with God's favor. They had met in church where he was the head altar boy and she sang in the choir. It was there that they strengthened their bond through six years of platonic courtship. In the religious and social life of St. Anthony's Roman Catholic Church and parish, the innocent couple found all they desired. They interpreted their past, stimulated their present, and planned their future within the Christian community that formed their extended family, and their little town of Dunmore was their Heaven on earth.

My parent's Italo-American, lower middle class, Catholic heritage built their feelings in a synchronized harmony, and the small borough where they lived, created a common ground for their basic values. When they discovered each other, it took little time for them to know they would some day wed and form a family.

However, before they found the bliss in each other, my father had known troubled times. He was the first-born son of an impoverished immigrant family, whose tyrannical father vowed to accept nothing less than his family's economic success.

"No second generation Rinaldi will suffer the same indignities as I," he argued. "It is on your shoulders Alex, to see that no son of mine will dirty his hands in the darkness of an anthracite mineshaft. You must get a diploma and pave the way for your brother and sisters. It is your duty."

Yet, my father had little interest in school. He preferred to be like his beloved Grandfather, "Thutaron", instead. The gentle, little man was my father's true hero. Even during the depression, Grandpa's energy kept the family secure and my father liked nothing more than to work beside him in the garden and bring in a bountiful harvest. That's what really mattered as far as my father was concerned.

The conflict of their values pitted father against son, pushing my dad into a silent refuge of safe isolation. Luckily, when he finally reached out to someone, he made the perfect choice. He found a girl who could gently guide him to inner peace, and that was my mother, his "Rosebud".

"Rosebud" Gaetano was the eldest of two daughters. Secure in a deeply expressive, fun-loving family, she blossomed with dark, delicate beauty and personal achievement. She was at the top of her class and her outgoing nature won her many friends, but no one captured her

2

heart quite like Alexander Anthony.

They were a perfect match right from the start and people sensed their special chemistry. Thus, it came as no surprise, when they decided to marry.

After their parents voiced some misgivings, conveyed their conditions and finally agreed to the nuptials, my parents exchanged their vows in the little old church where it had all begun. In the presence of God, they became husband and wife. They spent a honeymoon weekend in Philadelphia and returned to take up residence in Rosebud's parents' house.

On my father's sparse salary, the newlyweds enjoyed very few frills. But what did that matter? They had each other and that certainly seemed enough.

"We have it all," Rosebud noted to her spouse. "What more do we need?"

"It only gets better," Alex affirmed, and his words were prophetic.

In late autumn, Rosebud learned that she was pregnant. The couple just about burst with the news.

"I can't wait to be a father," Alex announced as he presented his wife with a collage of family baby photos.

"Let's name her Mary Ann," Rosebud requested.

"If it's a girl," Alex replied.

"Girl or boy, as long as it's healthy."

"And it will be. I'm sure."

For Rosebud, a first-time mother, everything was the baby. Nothing else existed in the world. Mussolini's, Roosevelt's and Hitler's deaths, V-E Day, victories in the Pacific, all paled in comparison to her conception and imminent delivery. Alex completely agreed.

The baby was due shortly after the Fourth of July. A fitting time for the family's holiday picnic.

"I'm sorry I have to work, but you should be there," my father said. "We have so much to celebrate. The exciting prospects of victory and world peace and the return of family from overseas. And our Baby! It will be a celebration beyond all celebrations."

Again, his notions rang true. The outing was everything my mother could have imagined and more. She could hardly contain her excitement as she recounted the day.

"Best time ever," she explained. "I wish you could have been there."

Alex took her in his strong arms and placed his hands on her bulging belly. "I was there," he said.

She smiled contentedly and rattled on until sleep finally came.

The next few days Rosebud felt too exhausted to get out of bed. By Saturday, she seemed a bit melancholy, but better. Then, on Sunday morning, July 8, she and Alex went to eight o'clock Mass as usual. After brunch, my father got ready to leave for work.

"Call me," he requested as he kissed her good-bye. "I'll try to get off if you go in to labor."

In under an hour the labor began. The contractions got closer together as her pain mounted.

She made the all-important call. "It's now, Al. Can you come?"

Alex bit his lip. "Honey, I can't. No one's here to relieve me. Sorry, honey. Better go with your mom and dad." His disappointment and frustration registered in his voice.

"It's OK, Al," she said compassionately. "I understand. I'll be fine. Get to me when you can."

"I love you, honey. Be brave."

My mother swallowed hard. She could not respond. She cradled the phone and began to cry.

Cries turned to screams as the intensity of her contractions strengthened. By the time her doctor got her into the stirrups, she was writhing. Frightening instruments took the infant from her through a dry and difficult delivery. At 8:45 p.m., the deed was done, and a pimply-nosed, red-skinned, hairless six-and-a-half pounder emerged. Her very own baby. Hers and Alex's! She smiled contentedly and relaxed. It was all over. The baby was here.

My father, trapped at work, finally burst into the hospital at 2:00 a.m. By this time, he had been assured that mother and child were doing well, but the faces that greeted him were almost unanimously unpleasant.

Alex's mother-in-law flared at him. "You did this," she muttered. "My poor daughter."

Startled by her remarks, he reeled again to the sarcasm of his

4

own father. "Big man! So you're a father."

My father's anticipated joy was completely reversed. What had he done? Loved a girl, married her, then sired their child! Why the purge? How could they treat him like this? He was almost too stunned to speak.

Then Pop Gaetano uttered the first kind words. "Congratulations," he said with a smile. "You have a beautiful, healthy little boy. Both mamma and baby are doing fine."

That was all Al needed. He broke into to a spirited run down the hospital corridor, where somewhere his wife and child were waiting.

So, my life began. It was many years before I realized the importance that having loving parents, a supportive family, a stable and supportive community and a strong faith would play in my life.

CHAPTER 2

The Problem

Picture this.

A beautiful, raven-haired, twenty-year-old mother suckling her newborn infant at her breast. Beside her stands a proud father glowing with the awesome awareness of his creation. Marvelous? Blissful? Perfect? It certainly seemed so.

The baby, now only forty-eight hours old, had filled into a rosy-cheeked, gorgeous little bruiser. He already was the nurses' favorite, their "Buttercup", all charm and cuteness and energy. Healthy and active, he kicked the skin from his heels, and his feet had to be bandaged to safeguard further damage. This was a football star or a wrestling champion, if ever there was one. My father was glad he wasn't a "Mary Ann" after all; he was much too contented with his little boy, "Bill".

During those all-important "first" days, the family spent a great deal of time together but, from the beginning, it was obvious that Bill was everybody's baby. Four eager grandparents, five surviving great-grandparents, scores of aunts, uncles, great aunts, great uncles, cousins each wanted their feel, pinch, hug of him, all too intent on ingratiating themselves to him. Their competition presented a stockpile of toys and unlimited attention, and by the day of his Christening, there was no room for any more outfits or playthings.

Yet, my Baptism was not about "things". To my parents and their extended families, the rite had much deeper significance. It brought me officially into the parish community, where I would be groomed from "boy" to "man" in the valued traditions of my heritage.

In "the little old church on the hill", as the priest poured the water of redemption over my head and put salt to my lips, I fidgeted a bit, opened my eyes and smiled. Godparent's Uncle Nick and Aunt Jean spoke my commitments to God and the Catholic initiation was complete. Free now of "original sin", I had an identity, a name, a presence all my own.

This was an important event, a significant happening worthy of note, and Rosebud diligently recorded every detail in the plush, satin pages of her *Our Baby* album. She enjoyed each entry that chronicled my steady progress and growth.

Baby plays with rattle . . . 5 weeks; eats cereal . . . 7 weeks; plays with his toes . . . 7 ½ weeks; responds to his name . . . 8 weeks; rolls over . . . 3 ½ months etc. The entries validated evidence of her perfect child, a pleasant, intelligent, hearty infant, fully equipped for the opportunities ahead. With such a solid beginning, I could reach for the stars and she was ready to help me soar.

My mother was not alone in her mission. The roster of relatives was a part of it, too. Whenever the Rinaldi and Gaetano clans gathered, they made it clear that Baby Bill was a top priority.

At Thanksgiving, Thutaron summed up the collective intent. As he stood at the table to lead in the Grace, he called for everyone to bow their heads and join hands for their affirmation.

"Le Wallyo", he began in his distinctive broken English," he is our riches. Let us love him and ask God to protect him. Each year he will grow as our families have grown and we will praise God for our bounty."

The family uttered a sincere "Amen" and the sumptuous feast satisfied their hearts, minds and souls, as they linked together for what was to come.

With Harvest Time passing, preparations for Christmas began and my parents threw themselves wholeheartedly into the holiday preparations and my first Christmas. My father bought me an elaborate red sleigh and took me on numerous rides over the crisp snow-covered neighborhood hills, as my mother filled the house with the sights, sounds, smells and tastes of the season. She baked fruitcakes and cookies, put up the Manger and decorated the tree. Its bright lights glowed with a welcoming warmth for Santa, the Christ Child and the well-wishers, who came to share in the "merry". Of course, six-month-old Billy was totally enthralled by all he could take in, and from every outward sign, the Baby's First Christmas could not have been better.

Satisfied by such a glorious time, my father and mother shifted their focus to the New Year.

"1946 will be the best year ever," Rosebud intimated. "We have to keep Billy awake to welcome it."

Alex laughed. "Our curious little guy thrives on late hours. He'll see to it that we stay awake."

Alex was right. Fighting off his drowsiness, just seconds before midnight, Alex put his animated infant on his knee and said, "Happy First New Year, my boy." Bouncing the child lovingly, he added, "You are my immortality and Mommy and Daddy will love and protect you always."

Rosebud nodded in agreement. Lifting a small glass of Coke, she toasted, "To 1946. To the three of us."

"And to a wonderful, wonderful life," Alex reaffirmed.

My parents, my loving parents, had every reason to believe that 1946 would be a good year. Alex got the raise he had hoped for and Rosebud started saving for my future. Providing for me deepened their parental commitment and motivation to expand their household. Carefully they weighed their wants and needs but they set no limits where I was concerned. I reigned supreme. My emphatic whims determined mealtimes, bedtimes and everything in between.

Grandma Rinaldi warned, "You are spoiling that child," but she was equally culpable. She, like so many others, was under the little rascal's spell.

With the arrival of spring, other opportunities arose to stimulate little Billy and to gratify me more. Captivated by the wonders of nature, I found my way through the delicate yellow- green grasses to play among the wild flowers and to hear the robin's chirp. By summer, I could speak about the joy I discovered in the great outdoors. "Flower." "Lea." "Sun." "Bird." "Up." "Happy."

I simply could not get enough. Everything became an adventure for my curious mind and my energetic spirit and I wanted to absorb whatever came my way.

When the annual July 4th outing arrived, I was about to become "one". It seemed fitting for the family to link Independence Day to my first birthday in a grand celebration. I was a symbol of their optimism; the Guest of Honor, the Birthday Boy, and my family enthusiastically indoctrinated me into their traditional midsummer romp.

The aunts showcased their tastiest dishes and the uncles mixed elaborate drinks to go with homemade "vino" and beer. The fireworks budget was expanded and Grandpa Gaetano bought a huge six-layer cake to feed the hungry crowd.

As he lit the single candle, he requested, "Will everyone sing my Grandson 'Happy Birthday'?"

"Happy Birthday," I babbled to his request.

"Happy Birthday," the family sang.

"Billy Boy" was one year old. Shortly after the light from the candle was blown out, things began to change.

Though I didn't know it, my parents saw my progress slow. Though I seemed eager to stand and take my first steps, my legs would not support me.

"Up!" I would plead with outstretched arms and with someone's assistance, I got to my feet, but as I attempted to walk, I waddled with my legs apart, tired quickly and fell solidly on my rump. Time and time again, I tried but failed, and my failures whispered scary possibilities.

My father and mother tried to minimize their child's developmental delays, but Grandma Rinaldi bluntly verbalized her concerns.

"Billy isn't walking right," she stated. "Something must be wrong."

"Every child goes about at his own pace," my dad defended.

"He'll be running around soon, I'm sure," my mom agreed.

Yet the stark contrast between my mental and motor skills built disturbing thoughts. To cope, my parents masked their suspicions with excuses, rationalizations and distractions. They allowed me to create a world of make-believe and feed their own fantasies. For their own desires and mine, they fostered thrills, which my weakening muscles could not provide. With costumes and props, I became a cattle-driving cowboy, a gangster-chasing cop, a floating spaceman, a swashbuckling pirate, or whatever suited that particular day's adventure and I was basically quite happy and content.

Yet, my inability to crawl and stand and walk could not be glossed over by deceptions and games. Grandma Gaetano finally convinced her daughter that it was time to do something more.

"Rosebud, face it. There's a problem here. Let's see a specialist and let's do it now."

Finally, convinced that not knowing what was wrong was worse than any definitive conclusions, my family arranged an appointment with a neurologist.

Since my dad had to work, Mom and her mother took me on a bus to the doctor's office.

The doctor greeted us warmly, asked a few simple questions, and examined me from head to toe. Then he put me on the floor and watched attentively as I tried to stand.

Struggling to sit myself up, using my arms and hands, I lumbered about until I had something to grab. Gradually I managed to get to my feet. With dubious skill, I took a few feeble steps toward my mother's outstretched arms.

"Let's see you do that again," the doctor coaxed with a smile.

The neurologist carefully studied my awkward style, as he jotted down some notes. Nodding silently, the doctor picked me up and placed me on an examining table, testing and re-testing my reflexes. After a disturbing pause, he spoke.

"Mrs. Rinaldi, I cannot be positive without further tests, but there may be a problem here."

His words made my mother wince. Their implications unnerved her. She wanted to deafen her ears and run, but she was frozen in the moment. Wide-eyed, she listened as he continued.

"Mrs. Rinaldi, I think little Billy may be a victim of Muscular Dystrophy."

"VICTIM!!" The word came forth like a nuclear blast.

"How can that be?" she cried, rising from her chair to confront him. "This makes no sense. A just God wouldn't let this happen."

The doctor recognized her need to be comforted. He took her hand gently.

"I may be wrong, Rose," he acknowledged. "The disease is not very common and I haven't had much experience with it. We'll need more information, testing, other opinions."

"You ARE wrong, doctor. It's not true," she objected angrily as she pulled her hand away.

Grandma, crushed by the diagnosis herself, tried to calm her tearful daughter. "Rosebud, the doctor said he isn't sure. We need other opinions. Let's wait and see. He could be wrong."

The doctor agreed. "Yes. These things are complex. It could be any number of things."

My mother took me in her arms. "I need to talk to my husband," she said. "He'll know what we should do."

Clutching me tightly in an overwhelming need to protect me, she turned on her heels and ran from the office. On the silent journey home, the sight of other mothers and their healthy children triggered resentments inside her.

She secretly asked, "Don't I deserve that, too? Doesn't my son have the right to sturdy legs, to walk and run and . . .?" Then she thought of my father, "How can I tell him? He will fall apart."

She dreaded that moment most of all. It would be by her lips and in her voice that the awful blow would come and she deplored her mission. When she saw her husband, there was no need for words. Her silence and sobs told the whole story.

My dad instinctively knew all that mattered to him might be slipping away. His stomach tightened. His jaw clenched. As he took my mom and me into his arms, our oneness bolstered his strength.

He said, "I need to know."

Mom swallowed hard. "The doctor had bad news, Al," she began. She lowered her head, as if in shame. Then she continued. "It's Muscular Dystrophy. The doctor says Billy has it. How could that be?"

"The doctor's wrong, for sure," my dad consoled. "We'll get a better opinion. I know things are going to be just fine. They have to be."

"They have to be," my mom repeated.

If wishing could make it so, my parents would have found a doctor, who could put their fears to rest, but every avenue led to the same dark destination, the same harsh pronouncements. Muscular Dystrophy. Degenerative muscle disease. Atrophy of the extremities. Attack on the vital organs. Death likely by ages six or eight, almost certainly before puberty.

Such grim statistics strangled my family. This forced them to make bitter choices and deal with decisions that altered their lives.

As medical bills mounted, my father sought extra work. Burying himself in double shifts at the bus terminal, he found the excuses he needed to emotionally withdraw from his wife's pain and his son's increasing weakness. The difficulties of witnessing our struggles were more than he could bear.

Mom, on the other hand, deepened the bond with me. She turned away from any and all that undermined me and sought a safe haven in faith. She believed that God would intervene and give me a long, healthy life. She prayed that the angels and saints would protect me and she would do whatever it took to insure that I would live and grow and fulfill their glorious dreams.

Mom enlisted the willing support of her parents for her great crusade and my grandparents responded tenaciously. They brought steady direction into my daily life and I loved their joyous sense of support. Each weekend, I eagerly looked forward to a fulfilled stay with my "Grandpa Beans and Grandma Fini".

"I'm going on vacation," I'd boast, and anything and everything became mine for the asking, during these special forty-eight hour getaways.

Better than any "surprises" that my grandparents might deliver, what I loved best was sleeping between Grandpa and Grandma in their big, four-poster bed. The ritual of Grandma removing her teeth and putting them in a glass on the night stand, and telling me mixed up fairy tales, like some gummy Mother Goose, genuinely amused me to no end. Her fractured accounts of "Cinderella" interwoven with "Snow White" and "The Three Little Pigs" invading the saga of "Goldilocks and the Three Bears" were a regular riot. Grandma tended to doze off during one tale, and then wake up with bits and pieces of some other, and I was simply overjoyed by all of her errors.

Grandpa, too, did his utmost to make life special. Each Sunday he brought me to the neighborhood bar for a frosted mug of beer and generous helpings of Chi Chi Beans. I joined in the sagas the men told and offered them senseless "kid" jokes in a dialect of "broken English". What tickled them most, and got me my biggest round of applause, was spitting in the big, brass spittoon near the foot of the barstools, "just like the Big Men".

Though so much attention clearly spoiled me, it fleshed out my strong points, reinforced my confidence, and fueled a passion for life. Day after day, I took joy in the moment. I was captivated by twinkling stars, awed by dawn and dusk, thrilled by babbling brooks and mountain streams and genuinely entertained by the sound and light shows of thunder and lightning.

I clapped excitedly as I watched puppies, bees and butterflies at play. Adoring music, I often sang myself to sleep and on rainy afternoons, I'd play the Victrola for hours. I usually fell if I danced, but I always managed to persuade mom to set aside her chores to whirl me about for the livelier tunes.

My eye lit up with excitement during radio's "Let's Pretend" and my imagination was as limitless as my dreams. Such untamed and zealous gaiety generated equally enthusiastic reactions from others and my playmates seemed to welcome my frenzy.

My aunts and uncles even fought to baby-sit for me or take me to town or for a ride. I guess I benefited from my status as an "only child" and the one deemed "somewhat special".

Yet, despite that successful level of interaction with others, the distance between my dad and me widened.

Clearly, he loved me, but it was hard for him to accept the fact that his one attempt at fatherhood was destined for doom. For him, the family name, the extension into genetic immortality, the carefree activities of father and son, became abandoned dreams.

His "perfect child" could never be the star athlete or grand achiever of his desires and he felt cheated. At times, his love got all mixed up with hate and frustration, not so much for me as for the cruelty of MD. That silent stalker let meaning and worth mercilessly slip away and my dad succumbed to the torment that slaughtered his spirit.

As he slowly withered, my mom tried even harder to preserve the family's well-being. She focused on the positives and stressed my abilities and encouraged their development. Stimulating my creative and cognitive skills, she built those strengths, which animated my personality. I learned early on how to capture an audience.

It was my great-grandfather who soon surfaced as my biggest fan. Each Monday evening, my Thutaron would sit in a darkened room with me and listen to my bilingual montage of adventures, both real and make-believe. That kept the pipe-smoking little man awake far beyond his normal bedtime, and when I missed any such Monday, my 71-year-old admirer would grow cantankerous and demand to see his favorite little "Wallyo". Nothing less would appease him.

I was his life, the fourth generation, the fourth dimension and the family's future. In America, this land of opportunity, I would be his pride. That was his mission. That was his plan. Ever since his arrival from Italy, he had worked towards a goal, where every tomorrow would be better than today and his gigantic will would see his family thrive before he went to his Maker.

Everything had gone pretty much according to his plan, until those threatening words about me confronted him. My father was his eldest and favorite grandchild, the father of a son that any man could be proud of, smart, handsome and well built. A child like this could not die! Thutaron wanted so much to believe this and he wanted Alex to believe it, too. To that end, he would provide symbolic proof. It was his way.

One warm afternoon in the summer of '49, old Thutaron asked my dad to help him plant a small Maple sapling. As if presenting a dedication speech at the erection of some worthy national monument, the old man posed, leaning on his spade.

He kissed his fingertips and raised his arms skyward. "Alex," he began, "listen carefully to me. As this tree grows tall and strong to enjoy its long life, so too will your little boy."

His own words moved him to tears and the two men embraced.

In the days that followed, the tree grew stronger, I slowly weakened and my old Grandpa died.

CHAPTER 3

The Victim

The passing of time made my fifth Christmas very different from the first four. My shiny, red bike sat unused in the corner of my bedroom and other toys were abandoned, because I lacked the strength to enjoy them. As my physical capacities diminished, hopes for the future eroded too and the holiday of 1949 hardly spelled "Joy to the World".

As antiseptic offices, medication, therapy and pain overtook our family, my childhood days became tinted with duller colors and my mom saddened as my carefree disposition changed.

"I don't want to see the Doctor," I rebelled when she brought me to the Philadelphia Muscle Center for a week of testing and therapies. "Please take me home," I begged.

I'm sure it was difficult to hear my pleas but she tried vainly to appease me. Yet, her efforts only made me angrier.

"I want my Daddy," I wailed, as I beat her with clenched fists.

Surely, she wanted my father too, but he could not get the time off, so she faced the crisis alone, like so many crises before. Mom was forced to handle the arrangements on her own. With faith and courage, she got a room in a hotel within walking distance of the clinic and she attempted to see me daily. When she was around, however, I usually acted up and the doctors said that she would have to stay away. It was our first real separation and a horrifying taste of what the future might hold. Alone and frightened, my mom realized that my fate was not in her hands. My future was God's exclusive call.

With desperation and humility, she found a small chapel nearby, cried, prayed, and dealt with seven long days of unbearable emptiness as she petitioned God for the life of her son.

At week's end, my dad finally joined mom and she cautiously released the emotions boiling within her.

"I'm so glad you're here," she said as her chest heaved with sobs. "This has been the longest week of my life."

Sheepishly, my dad kissed her forehead. "I know," he confessed.

As he wiped her tears, she found a resolution. With determination, she decreed, "Well, it's over. Let's go get our son."

The joyous reunion they anticipated of all three of us happily together again, quickly ended. In my own defiance, I bitterly turned away from them and clung to my nurses. Nothing had prepared them for my rejection and they were devastated.

"I can't go through this ever again," my mother acknowledged when they were alone. "We can't have any more children. It's just too tough."

"I understand," my dad conceded.

Though the admission stung, they shared a common understanding that their desires were secondary. My needs and wants would establish their agenda, and they would see to my happiness and peace, no matter what. To that end, they continued to encourage my whimsy and gave beyond their physical, emotional and financial limits to please me, but they would have it no other way.

Sometimes, however, in matters of health or safety, they set some limits and acted accordingly. When it became more dangerous to carry me to our third floor apartment, we moved in with Grandma and Grandpa Gaetano who remodeled their home. We lived at ground level and they moved upstairs. For me, the move was a good one, because I was where I loved to be; in a safer haven near my grandparents, my favorite play companions and lots of land and nature to enjoy.

The dwelling on Terrace Street was not the only new environment that fall. In September, it was off to school. I loved it from the start, a proud member of the first kindergarten class.

Filipini nuns staffed St. Anthony's Parochial School and the enrollment was around 200, intimate enough for a child like me. On opening day, with several mothers accompanying their children, the kindergarten class was a mass of crying, sick, apprehensive children, but I was one of the rare exceptions.

Excitedly, I led my mother out the door, determined to face this challenge head on. With characteristic self-assurance, I helped Sr. Mary in her efforts to calm the other five-year-olds and settle them in to their new scholastic routine. I was the old Billy again, easily in tune with the energy of academic fodder. Much to my parent's delight, kindergarten reports were glowing.

"He's a natural leader, a solid student and his classmates love him," Sr. Mary praised, and few papers or projects ever made it home without a star of achievement.

I knew, both instinctively and otherwise, that school was an arena where I could shine, and when the school year ended, I had the lead in the kindergarten play. My "Rainbow" poem and a solo of "Mockingbird Hill" were among its highlights and I egotistically basked in the praise and applause.

At the performance, Sr. Angelina expressed her eagerness to have me in her first grade class the next fall, but I never quite measured up to her hopeful expectations.

A rather significant change occurred in the intervening summer. In August, I got a severe case of German measles. High fevers kept me in bed for almost a week. The inactivity atrophied my leg muscles and I was never able to walk again.

When school resumed in September, my dad had to carry me to my seat and Sister Angelina, who had been so eager for her new pupil, ran from the room in tears.

I hardly understood her reaction. It hurt and confused me. My parents baffled me even more. They seemed to act quite differently since my legs no longer worked. They sometimes acted half way between "embarrassed" and "defensive". In their difficulties, I became aware of many strange behaviors. Ordinary methods gave way to the bizarre and a blanket of awkward arrangements took over simple matters. Just transporting me around became a controversy. My parents opted to use a stroller because that seemed more natural to them than a wheelchair but the stares of others soon convinced them otherwise.

That was a pivotal point, a crossroad. Things got told to me - about expenses and cautions and limits - that I had never heard before. I got a sense of their growing desperation in dozens of subtle ways.

I think that's what led them to the Muscular Dystrophy Association. They, we, were crying for peer support.

Once aligned, my mom and dad got passionately involved and found empathy from parents like them. They located eighteen northeast Pennsylvania families, whose sons shared the dreaded disease, and they formed a local MD chapter.

In the meantime, I more easily adapted to my wheelchair in a surprisingly upbeat way. To me, the wheelchair wasn't much different from my friends' bikes. I had a unique four-wheeler and some of my companions even envied me. They fought to push me around and I felt "special" rather than tragically different.

Reflecting back on that pivotal time, I think my dad was injured the most. On that first day, when my father sat his son in a "new set of wheels", he could hardly make light of that real situation.

At work that night, he thought a great deal about his son and the steel, leather, and rubber that entrapped me. It was an image he could not shake off and he was obviously distraught.

"Hey, man, what's on your mind?" His friend Clancey asked innocently as they shared some idle moments.

"You were supposed to bring me luck, brother," my father snapped.

The handsome Afro-American was taken off guard. "Hey, brother, whatcha meanin?" he probed. "I brung ya luck, man."

"Like hell, Clance. You failed me. You broke your promise."

"Why you talkin' mean, man?" Clancey continued.

"When I rubbed those kinky curls, you said I'd be real blessed."

Clancey made the immediate connection. He remembered the moment at my parents' wedding reception, when he invited my dad to pet his scalp as a token of future good fortune. Recalling that link, he asked, "Say fella, I'm a good luck man. Why you puttin' me down?"

"Billy's in a wheelchair, Clancey," Al responded, turning away. "That's the way it'll be for the rest of his life, whatever is left of it!"

Clancey was moved by my father's despair. He embraced his

friend in silence, as the frenzied sounds of the busy bus station engulfed them, and they cried and sobbed together. I think both men wanted to fix what was broken, but neither knew how to fix a "crippled kid" or a father's broken heart.

Little did they know that the victim would succeed despite the odds.

CHAPTER 4

Just A Regular Kid

Despite the limits Muscular Dystrophy imposed on my body, I shared the same wants and needs of most "normal kids" and, as a toddler, I eagerly sought opportunities for "parallel play". As I grew, my desire for young companions increased as well, but the mysterious abstractions of MD flamed the paranoid beliefs of many parents and they kept their children away from me. Even those who knew that my "disease" was not contagious feared that rough play or insensitive remarks could harm me so they avoided me, too.

The standoffishness, from otherwise friendly neighbors and friends, hurt my parents deeply. It pained them to see their boy quite frequently alone. Thus, in an attempt to provide me with companionship, they actively recruited my playmates. Through splashy parties, glittery toys, and the naturally gregarious nature of their son, they usually managed to attract some temporary "friends", but only one remained constant through it all.

When I was only two, I found the perfect partner. Her name was Carmella and she captured my heart from our first encounter. With a special chemistry that was undeniable, she provided the Yin to my Yang, the "sugar and spice" to my "naughty but nice" and we mastered the give-and-take, that built our bond. As children, we spent countless hours together keeping each other amused through competitive games of Old Maid, Cowboys and Indians, Hide-and-Go-Seek and Red Hot Hands. Our flare for creating a good time surfaced often and soon other neighborhood youngsters asked to get in on the action. So Carmella and I obliged with a rich variety of undertakings.

On the top of the list of such endeavors were backyard plays, which we conceived, produced and staged on Grandma's front porch. Following in the footsteps of Judy Garland and Mickey Rooney, we successfully showcased our talents and managed to build satisfied audiences that kept coming back for more.

As the shows increased in frequency and grandeur, their costs did, too. To fund them, Carmella and I developed a rather unique capital venture, which we called the "B & C Traveling Store". Using my wheelchair to transport products around the neighborhood, we peddled Kool Aid, popcorn and candy. We usually managed to sell out and realized a hefty profit. The easy cash encouraged other "traveling" business ventures and the traveling magic show, the traveling trinket stand and the traveling kissing booth, "a smack on the lips for just a nickel". These built the bank accounts of the skillful entrepreneurs.

Not all of our antics worked as well as our plays and traveling businesses and our impish curiosity sometimes spelled trouble. Given to reckless exploration and investigation, we took some dangerously frivolous chances, which put us at risk.

Much to the alarm and dismay of our parents, we unwisely concocted frantic flights of fancy that morphed my wheelchair into a "coach", "chariot", "boat", "plane", "train", "space rocket", or "steed" to take us on some colorful grand adventure.

We did a number of things to test fate and push the envelope beyond the bounds of safety. Among these was "the joust". Just like in Ivanhoe, Carmella would push me in a full charge toward the Dark Knight coming from the opposite direction. With long cardboard lances in hand, we, the combatants, would advance toward each other as fast as we could, the goal being to unseat the challenger.

Oblivious to the danger and pain in the "kill", fun, pure and simple, was all that we recklessly aimed for. Water guns, toilet plungers and other dangerous "weapons" varied the physical conquests, while I enjoyed the freedom of being like every other boy.

Sprains, scrapes, scratches, aches, and pains were a small price to pay for that feeling. I fought hard to maintain it since both my parents and other cautious adults tried to restrain my thrill-seeking nature and me with it. Their reprimands and warnings heightened my defensiveness and I progressively mastered alibis, excuses and cover-ups to do what I desired.

I came to know that real honesty could cost me, so I hid some of my less-than-honorable deeds. Sometimes I succeeded; other times I got caught. Once, for example, Carmella and I dared a companion to ride her bike up my rather steep ramp. Near the top, the girl lost her balance and fell to the concrete sidewalk. Boldly, Carmella and I offered nothing more than ridicule and laughs and she ran home and tattled. The incident grounded us for three days, but we weren't going to put up with that.

Angry and ripe for retaliation, I devised a scheme for vengeance. Under cover of darkness, with a corps of co-conspirators, I directed the trashing of the tattler's home and yard. I told my fellow mischief-makers to squirt the windows and sidings with grime, place boulders in the driveway and disassemble, scatter, hide and bury the lawn decorations. It was a perfect crime for the brazen ringleader, who was never suspected. I had won my revenge.

Other secret acts were not so equally well done. I got caught twice, when I spied on the "lovers", who were "making out", in a parked car a block away from my house. My cousin and I hid behind bushes to find out what the couples might be doing, but the parkers discovered us, and chased us away. When my parents heard what I had done, they were punitive and threatening, making it forcefully clear that they would never tolerate such "filthy" behavior again.

"Filthy?" I balked. "Why, I didn't even dirty my hands," I added with ignorant innocence.

"Don't get smart, young man," my father said. "You know what we're talking about."

I really had no clue. In matters such as this, I was totally naive. The taboo made very little sense, but I made it the fodder for future missions. Regardless of my parents' strong warnings, curiosity ruled the day.

Curiosity. Freedom. Self-expression. A lot to deal with as youth and an ever-weakening body strangled ordinary development. It was only with the assistance of willing partners, that I could explore, discover and grasp many of the glories, wonders, questions and conclusions of normal living. I found in and through helpmates, an extension of myself, and my arms and heart were open to them. There was one unfortunate exception, however.

When I was eight, my parents began taking a little orphan girl home for the weekends. "Julia will be like your sister," they promised as they welcomed her into our home.

At first, I bought their intent, but, as Christmas approached, Julia became a real threat. I had long reigned supreme in my domain. Now this blonde little usurper was threatening my throne, taking my things and getting some of the affection and attention, which were once exclusively mine. With cold indifference, selfish possessiveness, then violent rage, I tormented the orphan often.

Not wanting to lose her newly found home, Julia was long-suffering. She tolerated all of my abuse and my parents believed that I would ultimately grow to accept her. Christmas squelched that fast-fleeting hope.

After opening our gifts, we got into a terrible fight and an angry Billy was a biting Billy. Eager to force her to vacate my world, I took a solid mouthful of little Julia's arm and crunched tight. Heedless of her screams and the commands to set her free, I clenched harder and more brutally, unwilling to let go. This was a classic bite and Julia's skin was marked and broken. She sobbed deeply with pain, but I triumphed in my achievement. I had taught her a lesson. She did not belong and no one could persuade me otherwise. I was "the one and only". There was no doubt about that.

Now that my parents learned the painful and embarrassing lesson that their son was not prepared to share our household with another child, they attempted something simpler.

"Maybe a pet might be in order," my dad suggested, as my family calculated their options. "A cat or dog or something might give him companionship and affection and it might teach him a thing or two as well."

Though she always hated animals, my mom was willing to give

23

pets a try. She believed that somehow I had to learn compromise and unselfishness, so she agreed to open a zoo.

The menagerie of animals that found shelter with us began, of course, with dogs. Princess was the first of many and the perky little mutt captured my heart from the moment they placed her in my arms. I made her my constant companion and she gave me generous doses of unconditional love. The near-perfect match did what my parents had hoped, as I learned sound lessons of responsibility and giving.

There was much more for selfish, self-centered little me to master, so Mom and Dad often added to my menagerie. Unfortunately, other pets proved less successful, so I over-fed the fish, misplaced the turtle and strangled the kitten that tormented me. That's a matter which may have held far greater implications than my boyhood mentality could possibly comprehend at the time.

Much the same way that I did with my dog, I wanted to cuddle Whiskers, my gray Siamese cat, but the scrappy young feline had a much different disposition than Princess. With cool aloofness, the cat liked to dart in and out of the space behind the stove, scratching me every time she scampered away. In teasing repetition, Whiskers did this often with uncanny persistence. Unable to pursue my relentless tormentor, one day I finally snared her by her fluffy tail. As spiteful vengeance consumed me, I joyfully threw her out the window. Off went Whiskers.

Surely, this cruel act was an exaggerated release from my pent-up rage, a seething undercurrent of unused power equally strangled by MD. Much like Julia, Whiskers had become both an object of my hate and a target to combat it. It was a symbolic enemy that I could overtake and that felt mighty fine, mighty fine indeed.

Thus it was, that pets and friends and family shaped many of the attitudes and values, which cued my behavior.

But disability had its influence, too. Good and bad, ups and downs, hope and despair, tossed me about on a rocky road, a turbulent sea. To fit in to the mainstream and survive, I had to get through the tough times. Despite my secret fears, I felt confident that I would.

CHAPTER FIVE

Be What You Want To Be

Most children seek acceptance and approval and act in ways to achieve these results. In that regard, I was no different from the others and sweet little me tried to be what many people wanted and supposed me to be. I was a youngster who aimed to please and most of the time I succeeded. Since I could not run away from rejection, I molded and adapted my ways to be what I wanted to be. With the vigilance, support and help from those who cared about that too, I formed some healthy behaviors. An ever-smiling face, a pleasant voice, warm and welcoming gestures and an overall pleasant disposition added to my "good boy" style. I played the little angel role for all it was worth. That easily won over teachers, neighbors and friends.

Very few knew or suspected my more devilish dimensions. Only my inner circle was privy to the willful, manipulative youngster.

My parents felt a responsibility to corral their precocious son, but that was not easy. Muscular Dystrophy had denied me enough, they reasoned, and they were reluctant to restrain me more. To them, a child so limited by atrophying muscles and tightening tendons surely earned the right to release negative energies sometimes.

Their attitude gave me a trump card to play, so I capitalized on that and often tested their limits with tantrums and ravings. Lesser parents would have smacked such a little monster, but they rarely lost their patience. Corporal punishment was never an option.

They tried other techniques to control me: the family threat of the "little man in the keyhole", banishment to an orphanage, or confinement to my room. I never really feared any of that, because someone could always be found to come to my rescue.

There were at least two memorable times when I was unable to squeeze out of my misbehaviors. They occurred in the same summer, when I was eight.

The first incident occurred because I got caught playing "doctor" in the cellar with two neighborhood girl patients. To my Puritanical parents, this was a close encounter of the worst kind. My family was in trauma over my loss of innocence and they felt compelled to steer me away from the sins of the flesh. I guess they feared that unchecked carnal desires might build those fires that could not be quenched. They were determined that I would learn this message before it was too late. To punish me, they took away Fourth of July - the outing, picnic, fireworks and all. Enraged, I tried to get back at them, but no retaliations satisfied me.

The second incident occurred, when my mother gave away a set of my Spike Jones drums without my permission. She had no right to give them away, I screamed, and though she agreed with me and apologized immediately, I was not willing to give the matter a rest. Instead, I ranted and raved into a full-fledged tirade and mom ultimately was forced to call our parish priest to try to get me in check. The embarrassment shattered me and that was when my "get back dreams" began.

The typical scenario of such dreams was one in which I became angry over something and I felt the need to punish those who sparked my anger. Looking back, I've come to understand why these dreams, these spite and revenge responses, were probably defenses against my limitations, although emerging out of that darker side, was an effort to curb negative forces and coax the good to prevail.

That style opened doors for me which might have otherwise been shut. Being pleasant and kind worked better. If I were going to win friends and influence people, I would have to be "nice".

And "nice" is what I chose to be. Therefore, I was rarely excluded, especially among my peers. Active participation in a stimulating array of activities established many social links, so I focused on what I could do and did it with zest. Even in sports, I had some function, be it scorekeeper, referee or coach. My spirit and my mind served me well. Thus two-thirds of me was healthy, but my body, well, that was a different story.

It could not be denied that I was physically weakening. Though my parents tried to keep me unaware of the changes in my body and the tragedies of other youngsters, who found themselves in my situation, some truths could not be hidden.

Many mornings, I would hear Mom and Dad whispering about the death of another young boy with Muscular Dystrophy. Their valiant attempt to keep me ignorant made these times all the more difficult. The well-kept secret was no secret at all.

Yet, attempting compensation, we worked at "normal" things. That is partially why Mom and Dad wanted me to become an altar boy. Even though there had never been someone in a wheelchair to serve Mass, their religion and our church meant so much to them that they asked our parish priest, Father Tito, if he could make it possible. Father Tito surprisingly consented. He applied his imagination and changed certain ceremonies so that I could handle the activities within the Mass. Father instructed me in the Latin, and at age 10, I became the first altar boy in the world using a wheelchair.

The incident was such a milestone that Catholic papers all over the country picked up the story and I became a celebrity. My parents and our parish were overjoyed, but not me. I was quite uncomfortable every time I had to perform the function. It was frightening to me to be in front of large numbers of people, where I might embarrass myself by dropping the cruets, ringing the bells at the wrong time, or botching up the Latin. Yet it was expected, so I reluctantly went along.

Something else, however, conveyed similar notoriety that appealed to me more.

In the aftermath of the altar boy story, a regional priest brought it to the attention of Rocky Marciano, the world heavyweight boxing champion. The boxer soon contacted us with an invitation to come up to his New York training camp to meet him and watch him work out. Though I was never a real boxing fan, I knew what Rocky meant to my father and Gramps. He was famous, an athlete and an Italian-American. Thus we excitedly trekked up to the camp and were warmly welcomed. My connection was instant. I had a "buddy" and a powerful one at that.

During the day, Rocky involved me in everything he did. He talked me through his workout, a sparring match, snacks and dinner.

When it was time for us to go, he clasped my hand and said, "I'm not the Champ, Bill. You are. Remember that. You can be whatever you want to be. Just keep walking in your mind."

I fully understood his meaning, his mission and his challenge. Then he did a strange thing. He hugged me tight. When he released me, I noticed his eyes were wet.

Clearing his throat, Rocky added, "Believe what I'm telling you, Son. You can do anything you want to do."

"I believe you, Rocky," I said.

In the days that followed, the tale of Rocky and me got told many times. Dad boasted, Gramps bragged and our small borough took personal pride in just about every word.

Rocky kept in touch with letters and calls and we visited him a few more times. In fact, he even agreed to be my Confirmation Sponsor, but his manager scheduled some West Coast matches that kept him away. Though I was disappointed, Dad and Gramps felt it more.

Yet, Rocky Marciano's impact on my life can never be denied. He and MOVIES have influenced me about as much as any other force short of God and country, family and friends.

Ah! The MOVIES - my one obsession.

Mom took me to see Walt Disney's, *Song of the South* when I was just two, and I was hooked. The Silver Screen gave me all the escape I needed and then some. There in the dark, I found a magic world of sights and sounds and movement. Music and books took me half way, but the movies took me to another dimension. I was and remain a bit of a fanatic and there simply could never be enough.

If I partnered with Dad and Gramps over Rocky, Mom and Grandma were my film indulgees. At least once a week, we were off to see the musicals, the comedies, and the epics (my favorites). We had such fun.

Long after leaving the theater, I was still re-living, re-working the plots. That kept my creative juices flowing, fodder for so many hopes and dreams. Even in the worst of films, I discovered something I liked and I found messages meant only for me.

This is how God communicates, I thought - in Technicolor and Stereophonic sound.

Despite the MOVIES and the meanings, life sometimes got quite nasty.

For healthy youngsters, puberty is an important rite of passage, which marks the promising transition from "boy" to "man". That wasn't so for me. If medical experts were correct, my fate would be different, corrupted by Muscular Dystrophy's insidious power. The end of my childhood could mean the end of life itself.

Most professionals confessed that the prospects for me were grim. Yet, my parents held on to their hopes and refused to give up. They relentlessly sought "the Cure", investigating every channel, that might lead them to their miracle.

Stonewalls, blind alleys and false leads deepened their disappointments as the clock ticked, but my mom heard of a doctor, who had discovered a revolutionary breakthrough, and she was eager to explore his procedures. As she had done a hundred times before, she shared her optimistic hopes with Dad.

"Al, I'm hearing wonderful things about this new specialist in Jersey. His name is Dr. Geller and people are saying that he's helped many people. He's getting quite a solid reputation and I think he can help our boy."

My father's momentary silence made her continue. "What have we got to lose?"

Dad stoically absorbed her words. He patted her shoulder gently and said, "OK, Honey, let's give him a try."

I proved to be far less supportive. "Another doctor?" I balked. "I'm sick of all this."

Far too many hours of probing, prodding, and pain in innumerable journeys to doctors and clinics had eroded my cooperation. These futile, often humiliating invasions into my life, grew increasingly unwelcome and I vehemently objected.

"Why can't I be like everybody else? This doctor stuff stinks. It's just more of the same," I raved with hands-on-hips defiance.

"I know you're tired of all this, but do this for me, son," mom begged.

Dad persuasively offered his perspective. "Dr. Geller is a remarkable man, Billy, and you might even find him interesting. I hear he's like a Dr. Frankenstein and you'll love his unusual style."

The tactic worked. Since I had just completed the *Frankenstein* novel, this visit suddenly suggested melodramatic possibilities and that made this venture a little more appealing.

"OK," I finally agreed, hoping for an adventure, and from the get-go, I was not disappointed.

Dr. Geller's office was straight from a Gothic novel. Hidden in an overgrowth of weeping willows, its cottage-like contours, flagstone path, granite lions and gaudy green door gave it an enchanted, eerie quality. An ornate, bronze knocker hinted of what lay beyond. When the door opened, a thin Afro-American woman in a crisp, candy-striped uniform greeted us.

"Please come in," she said in a husky, Jamaican voice.

In a non-threatening manner, she escorted us to a brightly-lit room. My eyes scanned the numerous fish tanks, caged birds, unruly plants and abstract mobiles that moved seductively to the MUZAK. A pleasing scent of oranges filled the air.

"You need to fill out these forms," the woman requested, kindly assisting with the tedious paperwork.

When the task was done, she led us down a long corridor to Dr. Geller's office, where the old, gray-haired physician stood up as we entered.

"Greetings," he said, graciously indicating where my parents should sit.

In a heavy Bavarian accent, he asked a few medically related questions and carefully examined me from head to toe. Then the Doctor directed my dad to put me on a cot in a narrow cubicle, where a strange electronic apparatus pulsated.

"That machine will bombard the boy with special light," he

explained, "but the procedure will be simple, painless and short. When it is over, I will take saliva samples and a drop of blood from Billy's ear and study the results. OK?"

My mom and dad nodded their consent.

"You may wait in my office," the Doctor offered. "I will call for you shortly."

Without questioning it, my parents left me with the Doctor and his mysterious machine. Soon, the Doctor summoned them back. He placed my saliva and blood samples in a silver container, which was wired to a small gauge. Tapping his index and middle fingers on the container, he scribbled a few jottings, studied them and cleared his throat. He smiled with confidence.

"Mr. and Mrs. Rinaldi, I know what the problem is." He paused for their reaction, but they sat in silence.

Dr. Geller then addressed himself directly to me. "You had an undetected virus at birth," he announced. "When you were five or six, you had measles and a very high fever. That activated toxins, which your immune system has been unable to fight. Well, we know how to fight them now and we will."

He obviously struck the right chord.

Mom nodded affirmatively. "It was after that that Billy stopped walking," she replied, adding, "And there's something you can do?"

"Yes," the Doctor confirmed. "I can give Billy an injection that will help him. It will not restore his lost strength, but it will stop the progress of the disease."

"Stop the progress of the disease!" That was miracle enough.

For a family so desperately in need, the doctor's words and actions had stopped the clock. In that moment, nothing could matter more. Since my parents genuinely believed that God and science controlled my fate, they had been pulled and polarized by a biting game of "Truth or Dare".

"He will live."

"He will die."

"He will succeed."

"He will fail."

"He must be realistic."

"He must never give up."

So often, they wondered who had the answers, who spoke the truth.

God and Dr. Geller made them feel good and gave them a reprieve and a reason to think about the future. Now it was okay to forge ahead and cross over the bridge of adolescence.

CHAPTER 6

Adolescence

Adolescence! That dizzying, complex time of unwanted acne, Elvis sideburns, greasy hair, smelly perspiration and rapid, complex bodily changes, is the blessing and the curse of almost every teen and I was no exception. Through the grace of God and the unorthodox methods of Dr. Geller, I had recaptured a future, and this new lease on life allowed me to think about growing up and my missions toward manhood. So, with boundless energy, I became a product of my age and my era.

It was the 50's and the pulsating rhythms of rock'n'roll, rebels without a cause, Cold War threats and the Beat Generation sensibilities totally absorbed me as my teenage psyche pushed childhood out and ushered in the excitements of uncharted waters. Not every component of the New Age was painless or welcomed. Raging hormones and uncontrollable mood swings fueled my teenage angst and I struggled to sort out my confusions and steer my own course. Privacy and solitude grew in importance, as I hungered for the chance to come to grips with all that was happening within me.

I frequently begged my parents to "leave me alone". These desperate cries for freedom usually went unheeded, however. Dependency snared me, and I felt like a perpetual infant whose every attempt to carve out my own identity mercilessly failed.

With Dad and Mom constantly beside me, protecting, assisting, moralizing, CONTROLLING, I had little chance to set myself free.

To hold my ground, I plotted grand schemes, making symbolic issues over everything from clothes to music and movies, fighting tenaciously to win every argument. Whether by destiny or design, I pushed the envelope as the alluring "rites of passage" beckoned to me and I resolved to respond to each in their turn.

My thirteenth birthday marked the official launching of my agenda to taste the "forbidden fruits" and that summer I found my chance to indulge. On an idle summer afternoon, in the shadows behind the garage, I took a dare and sampled my first smoke. Bravely, wantonly, enthusiastically, I inhaled long and hard on a half-used Lucky Strike. My unsuspecting taste buds rebelled and my lungs gasped for breath. Coughing and choking, I doubled over with nausea and it took a few frightening minutes for my convulsing chest to relax. The deed was done and I felt triumphant.

I can check that one off. I silently tallied. Now on to the next. And that occurred just a few days later when drinking lured me in.

"We have a chance tonight to raid my dad's liquor cabinet," I told my Cousin Len. "My parents won't be home 'til eleven."

Casting aside any misgivings, I encouraged Len who was equally eager to guzzle capfuls of everything we could. Like two thirsty cubs, we matched each other, swallow for swallow, working our way through gin, vodka, sherry, cognac, Southern Comfort, apricot brandy and peppermint schnapps.

The booze sent us both reeling and I hardly made it to the bathroom before my stomach splashed its contents to the floor. Body tremors and double vision jolted me with wave upon wave of retching upheaval and the next-day's hangover multiplied and reminded me of the demons I had ingested.

The experience was enough to put a swift end to my interest and curiosity about alcohol, so I set out to conquer the final "taboo", the one that ranked highest of all. Among the Seven Deadly Sins, "Lust" seemed the most abstract and the most enticing. My parents and teachers shrouded it in mystery. They made it pretty clear, that it was something naughty, adult, off limits and that it had something to do with a thing called "sex". Other unspeakable four-letter words suggested activities, which were equally verboten and vile, things "only bad people did".

How exciting!

Though my parents warned me against sins of the flesh, when they caught me playing "Doctor" in Grandpa's tool shed, my curiosities lingered. I had to know more. The alluring mysteries about private body parts and what they could do made "sex" appealing enough to disregard their rules. With my body on the "Awake" mode, I could hardly curb my urges.

Determined to learn what I could, I found books, television shows and movies that offered titillating hints about the "facts of life". Starting with the dictionary and progressing through *Lady Chatterly's Lover, Tropic of Cancer, The Story of O*, and *The Carpetbaggers*, I diligently ingested biology, physiology and leering doses of ooh-la-la. Sharing my growing expertise with peers, I came to revel in playful, social, unthreatening conversations about sex. My friends offered me this safe outlet for my desires and our innocent banter presented sufficient initial stimulation.

Then things started to happen that altered the fun.

One night I suddenly awoke in the middle of a weird and steamy dream. I felt a tingling in my penis, a sequence of contractions and a spurting secretion unlike urine that saturated my shorts. Too embarrassed to speak to my mother or father about it, I allowed my uncertainties, questions and fears to persist as the nocturnal incidents increased.

With no one to turn to, I sought an explanation by touching and testing my body in ways I had never done before. Despite a bit of shame, it felt pretty good, and the satisfaction seemed even better because these pleasurable explorations were exclusively mine. However, my private, well-guarded secret didn't last very long. One night when Grandpa Beans was readying me for bed, he noticed telltale stains on my pajamas and gently mentioned his awareness.

"I see my grandson is becoming a man," he observed with a reassuring smile.

I blushed a revealing red. "What do you mean, Grandpa?" I asked sheepishly.

My grandfather paused, rubbed his chin, then continued. "Hasn't your father told you about the birds and the bees, Billy?" He asked.

After a cautious delay, I shrugged, "No."

"Well, you're old enough now for somebody to tell you about sex."

"Sex, Gramps?" I repeated, trying to mask my embarrassment. "I think I know some stuff . . . but not from my dad. Grandpa, can you tell me? You know how my dad is."

With neither disgust nor disapproval, Grandpa responded openly. In honest, simple terms he clinically explained the mysteries which had been blooming within me. He spoke like an older brother, a friend, a confidant, a counselor, and I gratefully understood what had never been told to me before: that I had a right to this rite and that somehow it would help to define some of who and what I was.

Grandpa's disclosures marked another pivotal point in my development. This wise, gentle, loving man established a common ground for me to believe that I could be a man like any other, that my sexuality was legitimate and that my individuality really mattered. In the dialogue we shared that day and others, I discovered another dimension of support and confidence and a comfortable sounding board for my feelings and ideas.

In Grandpa, I had a real friend. Unlike my parents, teachers and peers, Grandpa Beans passed no judgments. He showed no shock. He let Bill be Bill.

The empowerment of Grandpa's understanding, respect and tolerance gave me something to run with, it provided strength and muscle. It gave me "balls". Grandpa and a small pulsating aspect of my anatomy told me so and I wasn't about to forget that.

Therefore, words and self-stimulation were no longer good enough. The time for ACTION had arrived, especially since a young, attractive, buxom lady proved willing and eager to let things grow.

Molly was a zealous instructress, enthusiastically adept at "first hand instructions". With healthy endowments to flaunt, she had willingly showed all her "charms" to a mutual friend and since she didn't want me to feel left out, she gave me an even better show.

Since I had learned that "one good turn deserved another", my inhibitions disappeared as we formed an accommodating trio. The scientific "exposure experiment" in which we engaged, could have been a biology student's final exam. With rapid progression, seeing led to touching and touching led to more.

So, at the tumultuous age of thirteen, three naive "virgins" fumbled about to a sensational semester of passionate fun. Our scholarly studies and discoveries about bodies and bawdies and the forbidden mysteries of S-E-X proved that participatory education had to be the very best. I don't think I've ever acquired knowledge so fast ever before or since and this curriculum, in my opinion, should go on forever.

Thus, in puberty's complicated "rites of passage", my carefree youthful irresponsibility gradually gave way to early maturity and I successfully moved several steps forward. But, just as the turbulent waves of adolescence seemed to subside, an ego-busting incident occurred to shatter my treasured self-worth.

My grade school times had been relatively safe. They packed nine great years into a stream of enriching involvements and the final days promised to be the most special of all.

As the eighth grade unfolded, I did it all. I played Santa in red pajamas at the class Christmas party, was Civic Club President, taught when Sister Superior was called away, went on the class trip to New York and won many of the academic honors at graduation. A big family party and a two-week vacation to Florida were my reward and one final summer of simplicity capped a good time.

High school was not anticipated as a problem. Although Dunmore had no school with an elevator, the three Scranton public high schools did, and my parents planned to pay the tuition, so I could enroll. They were totally committed to drive me back and forth daily so I would be no one's burden.

But when my application was processed, I was rejected. The district did not want to assume the risk, liability and responsibility of a student who used a wheelchair, and they offered homebound instruction as an alternative.

The news struck an awful blow. It set my parents and me at odds again with the "normal world", shut out and devalued.

I hardly knew what to do. I felt cheated, unwanted, desperate and dumb. A part of me, just a small part, really wanted to give up, but my parents thought otherwise.

My dad met with the school Superintendent who, objectively and coolly, told him that the law precluded my admission. His professional, unfeeling pronouncement left my father broken hearted. He labored for days about how he could break this news to me.

Trying to make light of a bad situation, he finally attempted to explain our dilemma, but I got the real message and it hit like a bomb blast. In many ways, I think it was the first time I felt senseless rejection, because of my "handicap", and I was devastated.

That awareness brought a whole barrage of realities to the surface, the steel chair that held me, the extremities that could not support me and the limits that Muscular Dystrophy imposed upon me. I became sickeningly aware that I sat on the sidelines when other boys played baseball, classmates danced, ran, walked and lived.

I started to see how adults looked differently at me, that kids pointed, whispered, giggled and that family members patronized and sympathized. I began seriously questioning people's motives and my own sense of dignity and worth and my spirit broke into zillions of pieces.

My iron will to live was gone. What real future can there be for me? I wondered. Maybe I'd better start facing my fate. It will be no different from Tommy's, Bobby's, and Johnny's. Maybe they're better off; at least they've never had to face this crap.

Self-pity, despair, fear, unhappiness, defeats and hate took over.
Hate.
Hate!
HATE!!
For everything. Everyone. But most especially for myself. The powerlessness of my muscles linked disastrously to a corresponding decline in my spirit and mind.

For me, this was overwhelming. For me, this was THE END!!!
Or so I thought in the moment.
Yet - - -

CHAPTER 7

I Can If I Think I Can

With the door to a mainstreamed education about to be slammed in my face, it seemed like the bad guys had the upper hand again. When the practical, budget-conscious school board presented their case, they joined with an army of separatists, who believed that my life would be best in a restrictive setting. Even some well-intentioned family members agreed.

The only problem was that I knew I would be able to attend mainstream education and never gave up my desire to do so.

"Maybe the board knows best," Grandma Rinaldi suggested in the light of this latest obstacle. "I think the time has come to give in. Your uphill battle is taking too much of a toll," she advised her son and daughter-in-law.

My parents vehemently objected. Though overworked and often quite overwhelmed, they refused to succumb to the defeatists and harbingers of doom. Whatever it took, they would see that I would not be excluded from life.

"We have a victory to achieve and no diagnosis or statistic or obstacle will defeat us," my dad assured me.

"We've defied the odds before. We'll do it again," my mom agreed. "The three of us together are an unbeatable team."

Thus, with renewed determination, my dad went right to the top, the state Commissioner of Education. In a passionate letter, he told of the local school board's stand on my educational future.

"My boy is smart and motivated and equal to any other student in Pennsylvania," he wrote. "Why should he be denied enrollment? My son is an asset, not a liability, and he deserves a chance for a decent education."

Though the Scranton School Board's unwillingness to allow "a wheelchair bound student" into the mainstream kept my academic future suspended in uncertainties, my dad continued to argue, to justify, to persuade and just days before the fall term began, the barriers collapsed and another groundbreaking milestone was achieved. I was finally admitted. As dad rolled me through the giant wooden entrance of Technical High School, we knew that we had won.

Getting admitted was just part of the struggle. Tech was a far cry from St. Anthony's. The huge, old building and almost everything about it seemed foreign and threatening. Its faculty of lay men and women and the large freshman class greatly outnumbered the intimate "family" of SAS and all social classes, races and creeds shaded the sameness that characterized my earlier experiences.

The noise and chaos in the halls, lack of uniforms, a sea of unfamiliar faces took some getting used to, but within a week, I adjusted and happily settled in. I rejoiced in the fact that I had a place again among my peers and I was determined to make my high school years a solid foundation for my future.

Since no other student with my circumstances ever attended Scranton High Schools before, the Administration, staff and faculty at Tech faced the need to make several accommodations.

They first assigned a "Special Ed" teacher, Miss Smith, to guide my choices and build my schedule for minimum movement. She matched me with a young girl who volunteered to wheel me to my classes. It was a symbiotic match and Margaret and I became fast friends.

With my extroverted manner, my popularity quickly won friends and soon fellow students actually were fighting over who would wheel me around. Those battles boosted my ego and added to my confidence. Capitalizing on the acceptance and attention, I grasped the opportunity to fan the flame of romance. Brazenly, I made advances toward the perky lassies that attracted me and was pleasantly surprised by their response.

Limited experiences with boy/girl encounters and the codes of behavior, by which I had been raised, double whammed me amid this smorgasbord of new contacts and I whirled with the possibilities before me. Maybe my confused desires were typical of the late '50's and early '60's when passion and pleasure were all mixed up in issues of privacy, respect and purity. In matters of the heart, I gravitated toward the more demure girls, those "you could bring home to mother" and by that standard, I found my first high school crush.

Jeannie sat next to me in General Science class and we took an immediate liking to each other, becoming fast friends. Soon, our harmless, innocent flirting ripened to gushy infatuation. For a short while, the platonic mush seemed quite enough. Tech's bevy of high school beauties quickly tempted me to seek other conquests. Small talk with Kaye, love notes from Mary Grace, lunchroom encounters with Nancy and Marion's pretty pony tail and poodle skirt attracted me, too. Sue's bulging V-necks and short skirts quickened my pulse and Linda, Beth, Sandy and Lee even snared some of my dreams.

In whimsical girl hopping, I found an uncomplicated way to sample romance. Though I wished for more spice and the more daring escapades bragged about by other boys, the logistics of "how to" suppressed my desires. Thus, I kept my relationships light and structured my "dates" to avoid any embarrassment.

One incident, however, brought the unnatural absurdity of my "dating" into shattering focus and its impact crippled my expectations and seriously wounded my romantic life.

During my senior year, I met a good-looking, intelligent college sophomore through mutual friends. We unexpectedly connected in several common interests and spent hours together on the phone. We even met a few times for dinner. As our contacts increased, my parents expressed their disapproval and misgivings about our relationship.

"This is going too far, too fast," my father cautioned.

"She's too old," my mother said.

I insisted that we were just friends, nothing more. Objection followed objection, however, and the conflict finally exploded when I decided to take Claire to see *Irma La Douce*. At dinner that night, I announced my intentions to my parents, and to my surprise, my mother forcefully refused me.

"The film is much too filthy. You simply can't go," she said.

I grew quite angry. "It's just a movie. You gotta let me go," I yelled, adding, "How can I tell Claire that my parents won't let me go? It would be too demeaning, ridiculous, impossible."

"Your problem," mom shot back.

"You should of thought about that first," my dad chimed in.

I tried to reason with them, but they remained steadfast. No matter how I pleaded, they held firm. When every ploy failed, I had no other recourse but to call her and cancel the date. It was "the most embarrassing" moment of my life, I thought. Furious, I sat with a long face on the front porch stewing in my helplessness.

By chance, my cousin, Anthony, came by.

"Why the mug, Bill?" He inquired. "You look like you're chewing nails."

"And the plank my parents just hit me with, too," I added, launching into the whole bitter story.

"Well, you're not going to let them get away with that are you," Anthony urged.

That was all the encouragement I needed.

"You're damn right," I responded with a vengeance. "I'll show them, teach them a lesson or two they won't soon forget, if you'll help me."

I had involved my cousin in several adventures in the past and no coaxing was necessary to suck Anthony into the caper unfolding in my brain. Anthony agreed immediately to assist me in my nefarious plan - to stow away at my Grandparent's place for the rest of the day and let my parents wonder where I'd gone. The scare will serve them right I reasoned. With that, Anthony and I stormed through the kitchen where my parents were having dessert.

"Where are you going?" Dad asked.

Cryptically and defiantly, I simply answered, "Out."

Anthony wheeled me the five blocks to my grandparents' house. No one was home, so we took the Hide-a-Key and let ourselves in. With a satisfying bravura, we enjoyed the well-stocked refrigerator and color TV. When I got bored and finally felt that my parents had a sufficient dose of worry and pain, I phoned home for a ride back. I hardly expected my father's harsh tone.

"You got yourself there. You get yourself home. Quick," he demanded. For the first time, I feared my father's rage.

"Anthony, I think I'm in for Holy Hell," I said.

I braced myself for the worst, but when I got home, my parents' tempers had cooled to a disquieting aloofness. I sensed their anxious hurt and no words were exchanged as they put me to bed. In the nighttime silence, I heard my mother cry herself to sleep. Yet, despite my guilt, I felt fully justified in what I had done.

The next day I expressed my feelings to my Grandfather.

"I'm a prisoner, Gramps," I said. "Mom and Dad don't understand me. Their rules kill my options and I feel powerless. How can I ever be my own person?"

Again, in the role of trusted soothsayer, Grandpa gently took my hand in his.

"Remember, my boy, what I've told you before. These are tough years. It's a time when a young man's ego and self-esteem gets tossed around a lot and maybe he has to settle for less and give in a bit. Losing an occasional battle's OK as long as there's hope to win the war," he said.

"But the odds appear to be worsening, Gramps. Once it was great to be Bill Rinaldi. Now I'm not so sure."

My grandfather shook his head. He continued, "I wish I could tell you that life is easy. It isn't. Part of maturity is in accepting that."

"Grandpa, I want to be a man, but sometimes I fear I never will," I said.

My words made Grandpa turn away, and I knew he shared the same fear.

CHAPTER 8

Politics

Much of what other kids did in the ordinary course of their lives excluded me. Baseball, tennis, dancing, bicycling and other physical things shut me out. However, I was not thwarted by my "exclusions". Instead, such obstacles motivated me to find constructive connections.

In that sense, the 1960 Presidential Campaign became the ideal interactive opportunity for my active participation. With a keen interest and enthusiasm, I read about the issues and followed the riveting televised debates. The charisma of John Kennedy captured my heart and established my loyalties, so in the fall, I signed on as a "Youth for Kennedy". I immersed myself in the campaign, taking on a variety of roles.

At school, I spoke to the history classes about election issues, drew posters and sported buttons and hats on the candidate's behalf. I attended meetings, helped with mass mailings and phone banks and followed the inner workings of the grass roots campaign. The hard work was purposeful, important and fulfilling. When the Senator announced a stop in Scranton, I made his rally a must.

Just a month before the general election, Kennedy flew in to Northeast Pennsylvania where record crowds gathered to meet him. The huge turnout delayed his motorcade to the armory where he was to deliver his main address. I was among the 90,000 waiting eagerly to see and hear the Massachusetts's Senator.

As hours passed, I began to feel the effects of the long wait.

"I think we'd better get you out of this crowd," my father suggested with some concern.

"I'll be fine," I insisted.

When I almost passed out, my dad asked a policeman to find me a quiet spot. Relocated to the side foyer of the army building, I had little chance of either seeing or hearing my great hero. Outside the sounds of excited, loyal followers turned to sheer pandemonium as Kennedy arrived. Inside I ached for pieces of that frenzy, but like so many times before, I was shut out. Then an unexpected security change brought the Senator into the Armory through the very foyer where I was stationed.

"Senator Kennedy," my father summoned, "my son would really like to meet you."

Breaking away from the protocol line, the Senator went directly to me and I felt my smile light up like the face of the Mona Lisa. Kennedy stooped down on his haunches and traded words with me as 5,000 others waited, sharing almost ten minutes in kind encouragement. Then an aide urged him on to meet the rest of his audience and he was gone.

I guess the excitement momentarily dazed me. I can't believe what just happened, I sighed out loud. I thought, 'I'll never forget this for as long as I live.'

Obviously, the assembled crowd shared my awe. The Senator's dynamic oratory heightened everyone to a fever pitch and the armory simply vibrated with his energy. Kennedy ignited a fire and we burned brightly. He had me hooked.

Finally, after his long address, Senator Kennedy left the stage, exiting through the same foyer where I was still seated. He made obvious eye contact with me once again and began to wave exuberantly.

"So long, Bill," he said, and his hand continued its farewell until an eager someone grabbed it away.

"He remembered my name," I beamed to the excited people around me. "Senator Kennedy remembered my name."

You Can If You Think You Can

Each passing minute magnified that connection and by the time I got home, my euphoria had brought my temperature to 103 degrees.

Fearing that the evening had been too much for me, my mother urged, "You'd better get to bed."

"I could never sleep now," I protested. "I'd risk a bit of good health for something like this any time and if I could, I'd do it again tomorrow."

With so much drama in the incident, our Scranton newspapers deemed it worthy of the front page. That notoriety spawned many upbeat phone calls, letters and telegrams that afforded me a personal sense of "celebrity". Then, just a few months later, JFK was elected President and that was icing on the cake, a sweet victory for us both.

Bitten by the bug of political success, that year I went on to become "President" myself—of the school's French Club. The office called for leadership and service and leveraged my position to seek something higher. Friends urged me to go for the "big one", Class President, but I refused. Instead, I decided to chair the campaign of my best friend, Kenny Smith.

I worked as hard and imaginatively for Kenny as I had done for Kennedy. At the election assembly, I was sitting in the auditorium with the "Smith for President" delegation, literally covered with banners for my buddy. When Ken was declared the winner, I just about exploded. Letting loose a spontaneous VICTORY howl, I wired balloons over the heads of the other students and started a chant. Then, unexpectedly, I felt my buddies lifting me up, wheelchair and all, and carrying me down the center aisle to the stage.

I could barely think as someone blurted, " . . . and by an unprecedented special write-in vote, Bill Rinaldi has been elected Chairman of the Senior Class, a newly established office created by the Student Body." The students shouted deafeningly as I was taken on stage. 1500 high schoolers gave me a standing ovation, and in some ways, the feeling was even better than the Kennedy connection and I was hooked on politics for good.

Yet, politics was only a fraction of my active freshman, sophomore, junior and senior high school highlights. With ego, confidence and purpose, I got involved in almost every social activity I could. Yearbook, honor society and student council kept me busy, but my favorite extracurricular activities were reading for the blind and near-blind students and tutoring a mentally retarded boy. Reading held a special place among my interests so reading to the visually impaired brought it to an even higher level.

As they listened when I read, their faces appeared to absorb every word. They seemed to get excitement, joy and understanding in each phrase, sentence, paragraph and page.

My respect for great authors and great literature and the awesome power of words grew, but there was more personal awareness, too - about acceptance, perseverance and motivation. Through Marion, Tommy, Joe, Ann and Arlene, I learned that individual drive could supersede pity, that an undaunted spirit could accomplish great things, that by confronting one's limits and dealing with differences head on, handicaps did not deter.

These visually impaired friends had oodles to contribute and they did enthusiastically. Marion possessed more insight than a trained psychologist did. Tommy could make a trumpet talk. Joe had the lyrical quality of a songbird. Ann and Arlene's artistic craftsmanship found expression in a hundred unique ways.

My time with each of them expanded my awareness and made me grateful for the chance to "see" as they did; beyond one's limits to a positive challenge for growth.

Those lessons took on another important dimension through my unplanned friendship with another disabled classmate, Johnny Burns. Johnny, the retarded 17-year-old son of a prominent minister, brought home to me the precious advantages of a good mind and dedicated parents, especially since Johnny lacked both.

Johnny had a lifetime of difficulties. Though always well dressed and neatly groomed, his "differences" were obvious. His low-hanging jaw and open-mouth, undirected stare, lumbering walk and stuttering speech turned many away, but from our first encounter, Johnny showed a deep affinity for me. He often waited outside the gym to greet me and when I was absent, he often sulked away the day. He loved to do chores for me and his greatest joy was wheeling me around. No one could have been more careful, committed or proud.

One Saturday, Johnny's parents asked if he could visit me for the afternoon. Of course, I was happy to comply, but when the family delayed Johnny's pickup to well past midnight, it became quite apparent how subtly he had been parceled off.

How lucky I felt that my dedicated, loving family was always there for me, eager to help me launch and execute my dreams.

Yet the positive awareness, enriching contacts, and lively experiences of my high school years had a down side. Frequent illnesses built some scary setbacks to my plans and my parents' paranoia made even the mildest medical problems seem far worse. They persistently pestered me with a barrage of questions to assure them that I was well.

"Do you feel a draft?"

"Are you cold?"

"How's your throat?"

"Are you dressed warm enough?"

"Did you get a chill?"

Though I understood their concern, I felt uncomfortable when they fussed over me, making sure that I was buttoned up, seeing to scarves, hats, vitamins, exercise and often warning me in front of my friends. That was especially embarrassing, widening the parent/child gap and building more antagonism. If it weren't for Grandpa, I would surely have felt worse.

I admired my grandfather more than anyone else. I loved his honesty, humor and zest for life, his deep devotion to his family, his open tolerance of others and I wanted "to grow up just like him". Yet, the issue about "growing up" kept returning. It was still darkly clouded by what the experts said about steady decline and statistical probabilities, about boys with MD, who were gone, death and dying. These were private humiliations I dared not share with anyone, not even Gramps. So, I tackled my proposed fate alone, intensifying my defenses to hide my fears and weaknesses.

It was important to me that only my inner circle could know that I couldn't dress myself, go to the bathroom unaided, lift certain objects or even push myself around. Thus, I built elaborate schemes and outright lies to safeguard my image of wholeness, perpetuating stories to guard the charade. If only self-deception could have been that easy. The haunting presence of physical dependency frequently exposed me, and each time, that painful disclosure hurt.

My parents tried hard to spare me that hurt by refusing to leave me unattended, something I craved so much.

"What if you need a glass of water or a TV station changed?" Mom argued.

"What if something unexpected happens, like it did with that motor chair?" Dad reminded.

My answers were always the same. "I'd rather burn in a fire and feel a little independent. That's better than needing you around for every breath I take," I insisted.

The ongoing argument persisted until Grandpa effected a compromise. "Leave him with the phone and he can call Grandma or me if he needs us. We're only upstairs."

Thankfully the compromise worked. Gradually the frequency and duration of separations yielded some liberation that was long overdue. With freedom came several unexpected opportunities for all of us.

Dad started his own bus company and his fleet of six secondhand vehicles gave him a happy sense of accomplishment. Managing the line shifted his focus and he began to smile again. Mom took a job as a Stanley Home Products dealer. Free to set her own hours, she was still able to get me to and from school and have evening time for hostess parties. Her earnings were saved for my education and maybe even a house of their own and she reveled in her success.

As for me, the additional distractions that entered my parents' lives afforded opportunities to have friends over without the inhibiting presence of any adult "overlords". That helped redefine my options as a "typical American teen".

With less smothering and suffocating and a more relaxed posture for some personal choices, harmony appeared to be restored on the home front.

Two blots marred the happy picture, however - an automobile accident and the death of a teen-age friend.

In June of 1961, just after school let out, I was invited to the regional premier of the film *Exodus*. I had become friendly with most theater managers as an avid movie fan, so my parents and I were guests for the gala event. Before show time, I met Jill Haworth, the young starlet making her screen debut and we shared a live TV interview for the Six O'clock News. It was all so Hollywood - lights, camera, action - and I ate up every thrilling second.

After the movie, a gentle drizzle transformed into a pelting downpour that made visibility difficult. My dad took extra precautions as he drove our '56 Cadillac homeward. Four blocks out of the city, as we crossed the intersection of Harrison and Mulberry, a black Mercury came from nowhere and crashed into the passenger side of our car.

The impact threw me forward and I hit the dashboard with full force. Then my wheelchair recoiled and overturned, tossing me onto the car floor. My legs curled under me and I writhed with pain and shock. Mom, seated in the back, was similarly thrown forward. She fell between the front and back seats and was momentarily dazed. The steering wheel kept Dad in place with no apparent injuries. He quickly assessed the horrific scene. Though the car was totaled, his immediate concern was for me as I lay in a contorted heap beside him. Mom screamed hysterically and Dad pleaded with a bystander to summon an ambulance, too afraid to touch my bleeding body.

The driver of the Mercury was apologizing, crying, and trying to help. It was obvious that he had been drinking. In minutes, a police car and an ambulance arrived, and two young attendants extracted me from the twisted wreck. They pulled the wheelchair, bent and broken, away from me and carefully straightened my body as I gritted my teeth with each new position. Gently, they removed my shoes and watch and loosened my shirt and pants. They pulled me onto a stretcher as rain bathed my bloodstained face.

I searched my parents' expressions for some sign of how badly I was hurt, but they were both in a blank state of shock. The ambulance driver handed my things to mom who carelessly flung them aside. Unmindful of her own scratches and bruises, she clenched my hand firmly, not wanting to let go, but the paramedics loosened her grasp.

In the hideous exaggerations of crisis, minutes seemed like hours, but the ambulance soon took me to the hospital as I was passed from stranger to stranger.

"What can we do?" Mom asked of each.

"You can pray for his survival," Dad answered.

After far too long, a doctor came to my parents with word of my condition.

"Your son's fine," he opened. "His only serious injuries are a broken left leg and a mild concussion. But we should keep him overnight for observation."

The accident, its strange settings, the unfamiliar people attending me and six weeks of home confinement allowed too much time for all of us to wallow in the "what ifs". Nightmares of the whole horrible experience grew. Though we all had a lot to ponder, I guess none of us were about to share our thoughts.

Maybe a quick and merciful death is kinder than the possibilities of slowly dying, I reasoned when my low spirit peaked, but that illusion was soon shattered by yet another sobering experience. The finality, absurdity and wastefulness of extinction came tragically into focus for me through the loss of a high school friend. I can thank Steve Ambers for that wiser awareness.

In the ironic twists of associations, I met Steve Ambers in a sophomore English Literature class. The two of us surely represented a classic case of "opposites", at least on the surface.

Steve was seventeen, strong and healthy, with the perfect physique. He projected a James Dean image, complete with tight jeans and rolled-sleeved black tee shirt. He smelled of cigarettes and the heavy knuckle ring on his right hand spelled "super tough". Steve's hazel eyes hinted of something softer.

Steve and I shared an instant rapport.

When our class read Julius Caesar, I got cast as Brutus and Steve as Cascius. We gave our all to our roles. Like playful pups in an innocent biting contest, we chewed on the Shakespearean dialogue and the play's verbal tour de force was a stretching exercise for us. Gradually we found ourselves opening up our feelings to share private things, all the frustrations, disappointments and fears in our lives.

"I hate this bloody wheelchair," I confessed to Steve. "If I had your great looks and two good legs, things really would be cool."

"Think so, huh?" Steve challenged me. "Well, I got legs and my life stinks."

"Why?" I pressed with wonder.

Steve paused. I saw him tense. Then he bit his lower lip and began the explanation.

"My parents," he lamented. "My social climbin', ass kissing, money

51

making parents. They're so goddamn caught up in making money and social climbing that I hardly matter. Whether I'm good or bad, they pay no attention - no friggin' attention at all."

"You don't need them," I responded. "Look at all you've got."

"It means shit when no one cares."

"I care, Steve. Probably they do, too," I added.

Maybe he believed me. Maybe he didn't. For a while, Steve seemed happier because of our relationship and our ties grew stronger and stronger. Then Steve got caught having sex in the Nurse's Room and was expelled.

That broke our link and I lost touch with Steve. Though I missed him, I quickly adjusted to his absence.

One day, Mr. Walsh, our Vice-Principal, got on the school's PA system to make a surprising announcement.

"Students, please take a moment to bow your heads in silent prayer for Steve Ambers," he asked. "Steve's body was found in a motel room on the outskirts of Philadelphia. Tragically, he hanged himself."

The words hit me like a thunderbolt. Steve "hanged himself"? He was dead? How could that be? Steve was only seventeen and healthy and now he was gone?

It made no sense to me. Sick kids die. I was used to that. Steve was someone who could live, have a long, healthy, full and happy life and now he was no more. Gone! Dead!

That night I could not sleep. The specter of death had returned to haunt me and I was again blitzed by fear and confusion. What was this horrid force that too often intruded where it hardly belonged I wondered. Who sent it and when and where would it strike next? Why did it vanquish the living and steal their precious potential?

I tried to shake off these rattling questions, but to no avail. Every thought hurt and I felt empty and desperately unhappy. I prayed hard for Steve but doubted that anyone heard me.

Could a just God be so cruel? Would He snuff out a healthy life and come for me as well?

These questions consumed me and I wanted to bury my sorrow because it hurt so badly. I turned to my usual defenses - books, movies and music - but even they fell short.

Yet life continued and I knew I had to go on. I owed it to Steve. In many compelling ways, this was a decision making time, a time to evaluate my options.

I toyed with several ideas. I had no desire to follow in my dad's bus business or to be an insurance agent like my Gramps. I dismissed any musical aspirations after my guitar teacher made an insensitive remark. Teaching held some interest for me, and so did the legal professions, but they seemed too "physical". On "Career Day" I toured the regional newspapers for a handle on how Journalism might suit me. Many aspects of the job were within my capabilities, but going after a story was another matter. So my process of elimination went on and my search continued.

For answers, I finally turned to my respected mentor, Father Tito.

"Think about a clerical job," my priest suggested and I blindly accepted his well-intentioned advice.

The matter behind me at last, I could proceed full throttle to the glamour of senior year.

Momentum built to graduation. I got swept up in the glittering ring ceremony, class outing and prom. On Class Day I was named "Boy Most Likely to Succeed," "Most Popular Boy," "Brightest," "Mr. Personality" and Salutatorian. Also copping awards in Math, Science, English and the Rensellar Medal. I earned the PTA, Merit and NEDT scholarships and at the graduation ceremonies, the keynote speaker cited these accomplishments.

He chronicled my academic record, but his words ultimately turned my silent pride to rage when he remarked, " And all this because of a progressive school board that had the foresight and fairness to give Bill Rinaldi his chance."

How dare he give them any credit, I silently fumed. What a crock! My mind exploded with the injustice. 'They have no right to lay claim to this,' I reeled.

In my anger, my eyes searched for the beaming faces of the two unselfish people who rightfully owned the "Moment", my dad and mom. They had made all this possible. Their daily sacrifices, their hourly struggle, their lifelong commitment had never faltered. Now more than ever I wanted to embrace them and thank them and let them know that the reward was truly theirs.

In the flashback of those four years, I relived their selflessness, taking me back and forth to school each day, returning at lunch to assist me to the lavatory, being there whenever unique schedules or circumstances increased my needs, putting up with my rebelliousness, sarcasm and whimsical desires. They had literally weathered storms and defied dangers to get me to this point, while sparing no expense or energy to make it happen. They gave all there was to give to reach this day and no one deserved their triumph.

At that very instant, I wanted to shout out my emotions, but I knew my parents sought no praise or no rewards. It was enough to see their son on that stage, a living, breathing high school graduate. Their "Boy Least Likely to Survive" had become "The Boy Most Likely to Succeed." What greater glory could they ask for?

CHAPTER 9

Flights To Fantasy

Whenever reality got a bit too rough for me, flights into fantasy helped. Illusion became my tool for temporary respite and I usually managed to gloss over my pain and anxieties through my own resourcefulness and the cooperation of others. Many people, places and things assisted me in building a comfort zone for coping.

That began quite early on, and over the years, Aunt Ange's fairy tales, Grandma's bedtime stories, radio's *Let's Pretend,* Disney movies, creative games and role-plays with Carmella and my own skits and make-believe melodramas fueled my happiness. In the playground of my mind, I did all that other kids did and more. I imagined myself a running, jumping, carefree child in a bold, beautiful, joyous world of vicarious thrills and I traveled there often.

When I read the comics, I leaped into the pages, aided, and abetted Spider Man, Batman, Superman and the Green Hornet in their "quest for truth, justice and the American way". I became the third Hardy Boy, Huck Finn and Oliver Twist, or with the push of a TV button, I linked with Sky King, Ramar of the Jungle, Zorro and Rin Tin Tin.

THE MOVIES with color, big screen and stereophonic sound

55

blissfully often swept me away, too. They transformed me into a galloping knight off to slay some fire-breathing dragon, a death-defying aerialist bravely swinging above center ring, a dancing Fred Astaire or Gene Kelly whirling Ginger, Cyd or Mitzi in artistic fancy footwork, and all such musing was done with epic proportions.

Frequently reflecting on Rocky Marciano's advice to "think" myself healthy, I minimized my dependence on wheelchairs, special cars and unusual equipment and nurtured an image of self-assuredness. The reckless playboy larger-than-life, the roguish, romantic he-man, who always got the girl, the colorful, sophisticated bon vivant, who was worshiped and adored. These were my alter egos, but the darker side of my thinking was mine alone.

I guess you could say that my Fantasy World followed an age-appropriate pattern. As a "good Catholic boy", I conformed to the religious inspirations of my parents and nuns. With their direction, I got caught up in the dramatic stories of the great saints and martyrs. If I must die, I reasoned, how better than to go just like them. St. Stephen, St. Joan, John the Baptist and Christ Himself won glory and eternal reward. I vowed to settle for nothing less.

The impish, powerful devil inside me had something different up my sleeve. By early adolescence, heroic feats of daring-do set my agenda. This was the stage of attacking Indians, pursuing crooks, exploring the wilderness and conquering space. I saw myself as the intrepid adventurer or the champion out to save the world.

With self-imposed codes of valor and ethics, I designed my undertakings to override my physical limits and set high goals for personal achievement.

As I matured, real people - athletes, politicians or movie stars - became my role models. Their important contributions merited my respect, and I hoped to absorb their skills so that someday I could stand tall among them, a doer of great deeds and a shining example among the masses.

But baser inclinations were pulsating, too. Besides altruism, courage and social reform, other appetites kept boiling.

Seeing friends testing and tasting the highs and lows of romance, I hungered for a bit of the same. I wanted a girl, a "significant other", to call my own. Yet, the complex logistics of "how" and the intimidating realities of "who" made this goal seem quite unattainable. Thus, nothing seemed simpler than a one-sided linkage, a bawdy connection on a lit movie screen. As reel mixed with real, my fickle progression of changing infatuations placed my affections on Gloria Grahame, Susan Hayward, Natalie Wood, Jane Fonda and other beautiful or sexy Hollywood icons, but the ultimate love of my life was gorgeous Ann-Margret.

I was a high school sophomore when she debuted in *A Pocketful of Miracles* and I was smitten immediately. In her next film, *State Fair*, A-M performed a torrid song and dance number that drove me wild and I was forever hooked. *Bye-Bye, Birdie* was her third flick and she opened and closed the picture singing the title tune. Swiveling her hips provocatively as she persuasively enticed the camera completely captivated me and I took in the movie eight times during its two-week Scranton engagement.

That was hardly enough. Thirsting for more, I captured her further in a prized scrapbook of articles and photos and resorted to almost every means to add to its dimensions. I begged Mom and Grandma to steal pages out of beauty parlor magazines and Dad and Grandpa to pester theater managers for stills and other promotional materials. Within several months, the scrapbook was bursting and my bedroom became a sacred shrine of Ann-Margret memorabilia.

When *Viva, Las Vegas* was announced, I read everything I could about the movie and eagerly awaited its area booking. In anticipation of unparalleled rapture, I decided to stage a marathon viewing of the film by checking in for the first performance (11:00 a.m.) and holding vigil until the theater closed (11:00 p.m.). That might suffice for an adequate dose of my favorite star. For frugal me, that made a lot of sense - one admission, six showings. Twelve hours of sheer ecstasy-nothing less!

Of course, the idea seemed foolhardy to everyone else, but like Lola in *Damn Yankees*, "Whatever Billy wants, Billy gets". Throughout the day, family and friends shared shifts to see that I ate (candy and hot dogs) and had all my other needs taken care of as I basked in the glories of the great A-M.

Everything went perfectly, the movie surpassed my greatest expectations, and I was temporarily content. Every film, record or live performance that followed only served to deepen my fantasies. In Ann-Margret, I found my perfect female, an alluring sex kitten, an innocent angel, a distant goddess I could manage to love and adore, no questions asked.

When an opportunity to meet her in person arose, I turned it down. Keeping her at a safe distance forever was the way, maybe the only way, for me to satisfy my passion, I thought, and that would have to be enough.

Ann-Margret was not the only important "Ann" who captured a part of my heart. When I was five years and 363days old, another "Annie" came into my life. She was the first and only child of Aunt Kate and Uncle Don, and since I had no brothers or sisters, I welcomed her as my little sister. I loved holding her, singing her to sleep and indulging her in all the tender doting of a devoted older brother. We spent an enormous amount of time together, sharing movies, parks, picnics and joint family vacations, as she grew older.

I guess I had a very powerful influence on Annie, something quite mutually good. When she frequently turned to me for advice or support, I found purpose in her needs and pleasure in resolving them. That reliance formed a symbiotic closeness, which gave me a sense of real worth. It was through her, that I gleaned some insight into the female psyche, and that knowledge is important for any man.

Ann-Margret and Annie, one a woman of fantasy, the other a woman of real life, bought me a place and time to await something greater, something more.

In Ann-Margret, I had romantic dreams of happiness and passion. With Annie, I shared those dreams with empathy, fulfillment and trust. They provided special, never-to-be-forgotten moments, that found a nesting spot in my heart.

However, that fell short of all I wanted, I accepted the low heat of those few gentle sparks, but my desire for all the fireworks remained intact. In the crosscurrents of what was and what I hoped might be, this step was important. Without it, the gap could have broken me down.

My instinct for survival and the thirst to make life meaningful were deeply rooted and I knew I had to move ahead. If that meant a lot of wishful thinking and an overabundance of pipe dreams to come, then so be it. They, at the very least, provided some freedom and a path to my individuality. In the privacy of my mind, I could titillate my consciousness with all the allure and glamour that my imagination could handle. No one could take that from me. It was my exclusive domain and I had a genuine right to at least that much.

I continued to create my own panorama of possibilities. Like an ever-changing chameleon, I found comfort in the game. It was nourishment enough to get through another day.

CHAPTER 10

Thinking Big

A significant transitional year for the Rinaldi family was 1963. The catalyst triggering changes centered on my schooling again. Where, when and how I would continue my academic progress was a matter of deep concern.

Education was the ultimate symbol of progress and achievement in our household. The Rinaldi/Gaetano "immigrant generation" knew the sweat of their brow and the toil of their bodies was their only means of advancing. In their struggle, they built a deep-seated respect for learning and those who acquired it, seeing school as the pathway to opportunity.

"Only speaka the English and study study, study" was the mandate they conveyed to their children and the next generation adhered to the plan. They became citizens, got grammar school training in "readin', writin' and 'rithmatic," and grasped the security to seek greater things. Their sheepskin diploma held the promise to step higher on the ladder of success.

I, as the first child of the post war era, inherited the mission to move onward and upward. From the day of my birth, my parents planned for my college career. They committed themselves wholeheartedly, scrimped, saved, and put funds aside for my degree.

Medical needs put serious dents in their plan, however, but my mom's Stanley Home Products sales and Dad's promising business eventually amassed $10,000 to finance a four-year college program.

When the time came, my academic record stood on its own and several scholarships covered the full cost of my tuition. That freed up the savings for other things and after nineteen years of married life, my parents could finally afford a place of their own.

So exciting dual goals got launched almost simultaneously. Ground for a new house was broken on September 5 and I entered my college freshman year just four days later.

Though excited about college, I had no passion for the building project.

"What do we need a new house for?" I gripped. "I'm perfectly happy right where I am."

The tried and true was my comfort zone and 714 Terrace Street met most of my wants and needs quite well. Under that old roof, I shared nightly suppers with my beloved Grandparents, countless games of pinochle, priceless episodes of laughter, tears, joys, sorrows and unity. The new house meant giving up far too much.

The prospects of change, separation and adjustment to college upset me. Such rapid changes shook and rocked my confidence and requirements for college admission presented another threat.

My scholarship demanded a thorough medical checkup. I had already had too many of them but Dr. Michael Aronica, a respected family friend, handled my exam. Through each test, Dr. Aronica appeared more and more excited. After completing his work, he called my parents and me into his office for a conference, and he was beaming.

"The test results seem to indicate something rather startling," Dr. Aronica announced. "I don't want to over react," he continued, "but I almost can't contain myself. It seems that Bill has not had any additional deterioration or atrophy. The disease seems to be arrested, temporarily, at least."

The joy of that moment superseded almost any emotional high we had ever known. Mom began to cry. Dad jumped up to shake the doctor's hand. I smiled broadly as my eyes traveled from the tips of my toes to the ends of my fingers. Redeemable reality called back images from the past, the loss of muscle control, the childhood falls, knees giving in, useless legs, confinement to a wheelchair, arms unable to push, and my head falling back when the wheelchair was tilted. That all happened before the age of thirteen, then nothing more. It was all there before us, seen but unseen, acknowledged and denied.

"How has this happened?" Dad wondered aloud.

"Can you explain it, doctor?" Mom asked.

He had no explanation. But each of us had our own. Dad saw this as reward for my spirit and determination, my tenacious will.

"It's a miracle from a very compassionate God. He's answered my prayers." That was Mom's reply.

And I kept on thinking of the eccentric old German doctor from Teaneck with his Flash Gordon wonder machines and voodoo medicine. All of these and more had configured to make the impossible possible and we were given an extra-effective shot of new hope. It was cause for celebration and that we did with gusto.

What a sensational start for my college career!

We left Dr. Aronica's office confident that my physical strength could take me through the challenges of the next four years. Mentally I was not equally convinced. Tech had been easy, the curriculum quite basic. The University of Scranton was another matter, a quantum leap. It collected its all-male enrollment from the very brightest of the various senior classes across the northeastern tier of the U. S.

To be accepted, you had to have a good college entrance exam score, a record of above average marks and participation in several extracurricular activities and a genuine sense of purpose and direction. Upon acceptance, the incoming class then faced three days of orientation, a grueling battery of aptitude, achievement and placement tests and multiple orientation lectures. In no uncertain terms, the standards and practices of the college were defined with an emphasis on the individual's responsibility "to make it or break it".

Even though I was intimidated about trying to go to the University of Scranton, I did what I had always done, set my sights high and went for it.

Some four hundred 18-year-old "Frosh" shared the intimidating launch, I among them. Our common vulnerability quickly bonded us as we stood at the threshold of a life-changing experience together. That opened doors for enriching camaraderie and I quickly found many friends.

The college's physical environment proved far less friendly. Intricate schedules and inaccessible structures complicated things considerably. Despite willing helpmates to assist me, my dependency on my father was too deeply entrenched to tap them. It had only been my dad, who had taken me over curbs and steps or helped me with intimate elements of personal care. This was Dad's exclusive domain and so he adjusted his work schedule to accommodate my campus moves.

The first day set the tone and established Dad's presence as my appendage. Proudly, he wheeled me to the opening assembly, then to the aptitude and placement testing rooms. Though it was somewhat strange and humiliating to get about this way, I thought it best to rely on my father's strong arms and skilled hands. Any other arrangement seemed pretty scary.

College intellectuality frightened me, too. As I saw it, the competition included many very well trained minds. Could I measure up to them? I wondered. Were my study habits adequate enough to maintain the grades necessary to keep my scholarships?

I did not want to fail my parents in an area where they had come to expect nothing short of top success, nor did I want to destroy the golden chance to become someone of substance. My fate hung in the balance of what only I could achieve and there were plenty of doubts clouding my mind.

My misgivings and paranoia had validity. As the first student with a severe disability to attend the university, I was again encountering an institution that was unprepared for me. The Dean of Students and core faculty had virtually no experience with a student who had special needs, and my classes made little accommodations for a wheelchair. With a full-credit load that included Advanced French and Math, my confidence dwindled. I became a veritable bookworm to keep up, driving myself hard in the pursuit of high grades.

The compelling scholastic drive took its toll. I developed agonizing headaches, lost sleep, and overreacted to anything that lessened my concentration. Obsessed with the need for quiet, I put a pressure on my household to minimize noises, distractions and interruptions. I never went anywhere without a book, including the bathroom. One morning I got so engrossed in studying a vocabulary list from *Les Mots Anglais*, that I began to wash my face without removing my glasses.

That occurrence gave me cause for evaluation. What was happening here? Had I lost touch with reality and gone over the edge? I'd better get a grip or I'll lose it all, I reasoned.

Several fellow freshman were not as discerning, however, and the "mortality rate" among my peers was mounting, mercilessly sifting out the unmotivated or inept, and I began to see the fine line between "drive" and "driven".

Until the first marking period, I continued to wonder about the proper balance but three A's and three B's put me on the dean's list and set to rest the fears that I would "flunk out". With confidence restored, I slackened my pace and finally began to enjoy college life.

Much of my high school and college career ran along parallel lines. After the initial insecurities, I made quick but rough adjustments to this new situation, building comfort and contacts day by day. With a stimulated thirst for knowledge, my teachers encouraged me to think and speak my mind and that energized my relationships and let leadership skills blossom.

I loved the challenges and discipline that my courses demanded and I did my work well and on time. Some less motivated classmates often "borrowed" my homework and by the end of the first quarter, they fell prey to the "easy way" that ultimately caused their dismissal. It reinforced the lesson that hard work paid off and that college life had to be taken seriously if you hoped to succeed.

Part of the university's appeal was the rich diversity among my classmates. They came in a variety of shapes and sizes, interests and experiences, goals and expectations and I enjoyed the spectrum of their uniqueness.

For many others, however, the diversity tended to splinter the design for a cohesive class spirit. Factions formed as the rifts between "day hops" and "dormies", "Prepites" and "Plebs" deepened. Regional, academic or social class rivalries set many at odds. Like bantam roosters in a cockfight, they marked territory in some unhealthy standoffs and though the school administration noted the disunity, they failed to resolve it.

Since I had gained acceptance into most of the cliques, our Dean of Students urged me to orchestrate a plan of "collegiality". To that end, I opened up my house as neutral ground.

My parents encouraged me and extended the hospitality. Mom cooked up a storm of hearty, fun foods and a hot pot usually simmered on the stove for any drop-in guest. Dad kept the refrigerator well stocked with beer. The TV and couches became anyone's domain.

From Friday night to Monday morning, the household was jumping with youthful energy and lighthearted fellowship proved a boon to just about everyone and fed on itself. Gradually the campus factionalism waned and sounder bonding developed and strengthened as shallow boys slowly matured into fine, young men.

By setting petty differences aside, we evolved to respect each other through tolerance and sharing and that was an education greater than anything found in books or lectures by our most gifted professors.

For me, the companionship of male peers was like having brothers and I longed to be a part of them and their great and grand adventures. They, too, wanted to include me but despite the desire, I held back fearing that they might come to know my limits, my disabilities and my weaknesses and respect me less. Though the freedom to do my thing could have flourished with their help, I remained unwilling to expose the "secrets" known only to a privileged few. Yet, through the daily interaction with my friends, I fleshed out some new dimensions. At long last. I had the social and intellectual outlets for my inner psyche. Years of famine had given way to a feast and this was just the appetizer. Fate soon offered a sumptuous first course.

As a family-minded young man, I was ripe for kids, young ones who needed me as much as I needed them. I found the perfect opportunity through some young cousins, the four McHales.

Their mother was my Aunt Ange. She had always been quite special to me. When I was an infant, she frequently baby-sat. She read me fairy tales, taught me to play Poker and guided my youthful hands as I learned to draw.

Life got somewhat derailed for her and after a turbulent ten-year marriage, Aunt Ange faced the difficulties of raising four children alone. She had moved away to Baltimore when the first baby was born. Now with three more and no husband to support them, Aunt Ange was in trouble. Reluctantly, she brought her beautiful brood back to Dunmore so we could lend a hand.

The children were our joy. Each had a "special something" to engage us. Carole, the oldest child and only girl, was cute and intelligent. She had an affectionate nature and tender inner warmth, a little mother to her brothers.

Greg came second - blond, blue-eyed, energetic - a bald, smiling and bubbly baby, who grew into a muscular, athletic little boy. Fishing, hunting, baseball and the total spectrum of sports and physical activities preoccupied his attention.

Don, the second son, was a real tiger with striped hair to boot. He had a fighting, independent nature and a quick, alert mind.

Richard, the baby of the bunch, was the most beautiful with curly, red hair and haunting green eyes. His docile, cheery nature made him eager to reach out to embracing arms and this he did with charming regularity.

After Aunt Ange returned from Baltimore, I spent countless hours with her kids. Each brought out qualities in me that greatly satisfied my paternal instincts and gave me a very different perspective, one directed to the care and direction of others. With college life to stimulate my mind, the McHale children were present to satisfy my heart.

What an exhilarating blueprint for happiness!

But, just as the good things gelled and my spirit soared, a bullet in Dallas burst my bubble with cruel sobriety. On that fateful Friday in November, Death intruded again. From out of the blue, it struck another blow, viciously shattering the prospects for on-going inner peace. I could have never guessed the events of that sunny autumn day. My friend, Bob Kearney, and I were reviewing for a French quiz when frenzied shouts startled us.

"The President's been shot," a student yelled to anyone who would listen.

"Another hazing carryover," Bob guessed. "Another silly prank."

"Not very funny," I added with annoyance.

In minutes, excited groups began to cluster and Bob and I made it over to a car radio to hear the fast-developing news.

"The President has been gunned down in a Dallas motorcade. It is believed that he has D-I-E-D!"

The details continued as the President's fate ultimately unfolded.

In some distant place, by some unknown force, Death had struck again and a great man was gone.

The confirmation stung like an electric shock. I felt sick and empty inside. The man I so admired, worked for and met, had just been slaughtered - the victim of an anonymous killer.

Suddenly images of the dead flooded my brain. Thutaron! Steve Anders! My young MD "brothers" - Tommy, Bobby, Johnny! The high-minded President! Gallows. Guillotines. Firing squads. Mayhem. Murder. D-E-A-T-H.

Bitter thoughts and threats returned. Death and its abstract mysteries, its annihilations, its separations, its sorrows, its POWER - back again and victorious.

Thutaron was old. Steve was desperate. Tommy, Bobby and Johnny were "sick". But JFK? He symbolized hope, vitality, and achievement. Now stalking "Death", the relentless, remorseless Killer had claimed even him.

To me, this God-awful force was like none other. It could take you on, rape and rob you and destroy all you had worked to achieve and there was not a single thing you could do to prevent it. It made life ridiculous and futile as it claimed the very best and denied the world of its great potential.

This ULTIMATE CONQUEROR. Where would it strike next?

In less than a year, I would have the mocking answer. Bob Kearney would be gone, too - the victim of a rare kidney disease. To my college friends in the prime of their lives, Bob's death was unfathomable. I had been over this rugged terrain far too many times. I knew what it was like to see the young pass on as surely as the old, that there was no age of invincibility. It was my mission to tell them that and make them understand and maybe, in this atmosphere of learned men, they could grasp a purpose for it all. Learned professors, platitudinous Philosophy courses, endless scholarly discussions and provocative debates hardly mattered; the mystery remained intact. I understood the pain. That I could feel - deeply. But the "Why" was another matter, a matter I needed to resolve.

Simple, pat answers failed me miserably.

My mother's early training said, "A kind and just God exists, who has His own reasons for the way things are."

The good nuns at St. Anthony's and the dedicated parish priests taught equally blind acceptance of these troubling abstractions and I had bought their rationalizations, holding firm in my faith.

Now my mind wanted more. My doubts turned me off and away - not from God, but from all the structure and organization of traditional beliefs. I got no comfort from that. Sunday Mass held little meaning and I began skipping the sacraments as skepticism and aloofness set me apart.

My changed attitude and actions greatly disturbed my mother and, for the first time, we had an issue that deeply divided us. To my parents, the church was a lifeline. Dad had dutifully taken me to Sunday Mass since I was an infant. There I was baptized, confessed and confirmed. I served as an altar boy and actively participated in ceremonies and rituals of spiritual growth. My parents and I were even compared to the "Holy Family" incarnate, a pastoral example of solid faith and Catholic values.

But, on the very brink of adulthood, I found wide gaps in my beliefs. The worship that my parents held sacred seemed meaningless to me and I felt like a hypocrite. As my spiritual identity deteriorated, my thoughts on my eternal destiny shattered with bewilderment. I sought an objective listener to sort it all out, but on this delicate topic, Grandpa offered little insight. Father Tito was just too close to the situation to do me any good. My Jesuit teachers spoke too ethereally for these practical needs and my peers seemed equally confused. So my uncertainties continued.

Since the matter would not go away, I mustered up the courage to phone an anonymous clergyman to express my feelings. Instead of compassion, I got only his annoyance and indifference. Cradling the phone with disgust, I was ready to cast aside the whole mission.

Why did I need formal religion anyway, I questioned? Church sacraments, rites, ceremonies, earthly mediators to the Divine Presence can't really matter. God lives in me and this one-to-one experience should be enough.

In that reasoning, I vowed to let my destiny be a product of my own making. On the profound issues like life and death and every other matter that lay ahead, I decided to find the real answers, the dependable solutions, if they existed at all, from within myself.

Out there on that limb, unprotected and unassisted, I set out again to rediscover who and what I was. The protective bubble, in which I had lived, afforded too few opportunities for self-definition. There had to be more exercises, more tests of internal awareness and I resolved to unleash them, whenever and wherever, they might be.

Pushing the envelope, I threw cautions aside and brashly asserted my desires to learn about everything my curiosity demanded. "The forbidden" became the sirens' call seducing me toward discovery as I pursued my quest for the unknown. Vicariously or by direct immersion, I vowed to find my identity at last.

Again, the REAL and the REEL provided fodder for understanding. Having outgrown Disney, bolder, more adult movies beckoned. *Blow-Up*, the condemned but acclaimed Antonioni film, got a Scranton booking. The incident was surrounded with controversy when the Bishop sent letters to all parishes urging the Diocesan population to boycott the film and any theater that showed it. As the intellectual circles were saying, "See it!" The Church was warning, "Don't!"

My personal curiosities and my position as film reviewer for the University of Scranton's newspaper deepened my interest in the film. The weekly column with its flagrant style had groomed a readership that respected my challenges to the school's administration. Their earlier objections to the "double entendres" of my *Marriage, Italian Style* review sparked a heated controversy over censorship and freedoms of speech and press and the matter almost led to my expulsion. When my writings finally went to press intact, my "victory over the Establishment" came to represent a conquest for campus student rights.

So *Blow-Up* held the potential to build my reputation and my review would be my stand. But, to write about the film, I had to see it and that was the rub.

Mom and Dad had dutifully taken their Legion of Decency pledge against the movie. I, on the other hand, refused, and set a very deliberate course to see the "nudity-riddled" Antonioni Classic.

When my parents expressed a firm "no", it was shades of *Irma La Douce* all over again. This time I was a college thinker with "weapons" of wit and logic in my arsenal.

"It is my duty as campus film critic to review the movie," I argued.

69

"I'm a man now, you know. Twenty-year-olds shouldn't be tied to parents' outdated, narrow-minded moral codes."

"Our house, our rules," they insisted.

"What's the big deal?" I countered. "A flash of nudity and a glimpse of kinky sex never hurt anybody."

Yep! I had spoken the "S" word and the mere mention of exposed skin on the silver screen was enough to defeat me. Even as I spoke, I knew I had breached a cardinal taboo.

So, I attempted a different means. "You're making me a prisoner, of your power and your values," I objected. "You keep me jailed up in your strict, prissy beliefs. That just isn't fair."

"Fair or not, we've made a pledge," Mom responded.

"Your pledge. Not mine. If I could take myself, I wouldn't have to beg. Is that what I have to do? Beg - like a lap dog."

That struck the chord I had hoped for. The enemy was foiled again. The next day they dropped me off at the theater. *Blow Up* was a disappointment, boring and much too arty for my tastes, but I had won another small victory in the big war - the ongoing fight to be myself, whatever that "myself" might be.

As other incidents cropped up, each new experience brought lessons of greater personal insight for me. Increasingly self-assured, I branched out to more prominent pursuits. The recognition and popularity of my weekly column broadened my spheres of influence. I joined the university's literary magazine, yearbook, and Business Club, and earned highest honors in Theology and Business. By the end of my sophomore year, I was inducted into Alpha Sigma Nu, the Jesuit Honor Society.

With such credits to my name, my friends saw my chance to hold a class office. Believing that I could crack the power structure which had long-dominated student government, they goaded me into campus politics. Through their persuasion, I tossed my hat in the ring. The fond memories of past political experiences whetted my desire for the new venture, but I set my sights on a low-level office.

"If you're going to get involved, go for something big," my father advised.

He knew I was always up to any challenge. He also knew my

chances were good since he spent so much time on campus. "You can get elected to almost any office," he encouraged and many others supported that belief.

Frank Rudegair, my closest college friend, signed on as my campaign manager, circulating petitions for "Student Body Vicepresident" under the Progressive Party banner. The office held policymaking power on campus, making the challenge a formidable one. After the Election Board reviewed my credentials and accepted my petition, the campaign officially began in earnest.

In the two-tiered election process, I had to face two rather weak candidates in a rather dull Primary. In that phase, an easy victory was almost a foregone conclusion. But the general election posed a much stiffer competition. The Conservatives had a powerful incumbent as their standard bearer. He had already won decisive victories before so our strategy was to enhance my name recognition and attract attention with clever slogans, posters and name cards. The crucial impact was sure to be the "Candidates Debate."

I was determined to impress the audience with the best I had to offer. Psyching myself for the oratory and putting misgivings and uneasiness aside, I found the tenacity that was waiting in reserve and confidently traded verbal interchanges with my opponent. My Dad beamed as he witnessed the reactions around him. Everyone sensed that this was going to be a tight race.

On election day, the polls opened in the early morning. Each minute exaggerated my tensions, making it difficult to concentrate on my classes. By noon, my anxieties had peaked and I needed some relief. Cutting the remainder of my classes, I retreated to an Ann-Margret movie where my celluloid love goddess worked her Cinemascope magic to soothe me. After the movie, I went home to await the results. Though the wait was brief, it seemed forever. Around eight, the phone rang and I excitedly picked up the receiver for the news.

Frank's bland "Hello" gave no clue. Even his first words left the outcome dangling. "You made a good showing, and you can be real proud," Frank toyed.

I couldn't stand it. "Frank; spit it out," I demanded. "Did I make it?"

"Of course, Mr. VP. You killed 'em. We're on our way up. Crack out the champagne. It's celebration time." Wow! Wow!! Wow!!! I had beaten the odds again. The "Boy Least Likely to Survive" had chalked up another V-I-C-T-O-R-Y.

Now, what was next?

Where did I go from here???

CHAPTER 11

The World Of Work

As my college years drew to a close, the bigger, more competitive work world loomed ahead and people voiced optimistic notions regarding my future.

"You've done so well," Mom noted, "that I'm sure you'll find a good job right after graduation."

Father Tito reinforced her belief. "Firms are always on the lookout for accountants. Just scour the ads," he suggested.

Dad saw things differently. He was frightened by the competitive nature of free enterprise so he thought I should become the manager of his bus line.

"I can use your help," he suggested. "We can make the company succeed if we do it together."

I saw little hope in that option. The venture had fallen on hard times. Dad's busses were in poor shape and beyond repair. His drivers grew indifferent and surly. Loyal riders gradually found other means of transportation. Bill collectors became harsher and more threatening with each passing day. Mom tried to persuade my dad to abandon the sinking ship, but he vehemently refused.

"We need this business. It's our son's future," he insisted.

The declining business triggered arguments and bitter words. Yet, Dad refused to give the business up. It simply meant too much to him - his hope, the future of his family. If it failed, he failed. If it died, what else might there be?

The vulnerability of the bus business and its parallels to life in the Rinaldi family presented a compelling comparison and contrast to me. It begged the questions of when to hold and when to fold, when to give in and when to give up. Though we had usually supported each other through most of our struggles and complications, the Suburban Transit Company set us at odds. Mom and Dad fought over our future and our security.

Their marriage faltered and the household upheaval rocked me, too.

As my parental loyalties shifted from one parent to the other, for the first time, my grades fell off and other issues fueled turmoil and chaos.

DEATH, that sobering, omnipresent force, ultimately and ironically restored order and put everything in its proper perspective. Though unwelcome and unwanted, the Grim Reaper re-emerged and with its anguishing strength came catharsis, purification and escape. This time its victim, its sacrificial lamb, was my namesake, Grandpa Rinaldi.

Grandpa Rinaldi had once been a giant, a mighty man with a robust body and a tenacious will. Poverty, alcohol and a coal miner's life changed all that. Irregular hours, a poor diet and a life of constant work had taken its toll. Black lung disease taxed his heart, broke, and bent his frame. He was old beyond his years, but though life's drudgery had soured his disposition, his character was clean and he lived as unselfishly as any man could.

When I, his first grandchild was born, his hopes ran high that the family name would go on and rise to greater status. My "condition" put a damper on that. With a business in the "Rinaldi" name failing, too, it was more than Grandpa could bear. Disappointed, discouraged and disgruntled, I think he made a deal with the Devil for an exit from his pain. So he died as he had lived, in surging gasps and grimaces with the bitter taste of life in his mouth.

Had he fought for just a few more months, Grandpa would have seen his son give up the damaging business and his oldest grandchild, his namesake, become the first Rinaldi to obtain a college degree.

Maybe it was the sacrifice of his life, which motivated his family to go forward again, to grasp another beginning in the unending cycle of rebirth and renewal.

A week after Grandpa's funeral, I graduated from college, the culmination of four productive years. Capped, gowned, and hooded among three hundred scholarly young men, I proudly took my place in the mainstream, in a vanguard that held the promise of tomorrow in our hands.

Filled with optimism, I began in earnest to search for a job in our area. After several interviews, I finally heard from RCA. There I took a stiff battery of tests and afterwards I met with the personnel director to discuss the results.

"Well, young man," the executive opened in a businesslike voice, "from the evidence we have before us, we can see that your college and high school grades reflect a very true picture. Your test scores are the highest we've ever had. Congratulations, my boy."

His words pleased and encouraged me, but the happy feelings were very short-lived when the interviewer asked, "Can you work a Stat machine?"

Though I had some training in the use of a few calculators, this plant's machines required someone to stand to run them.

Since I couldn't do that, the executive reluctantly explained, "Then we cannot use you. You are unsuited for the job."

Though somewhat disappointed, I quickly set out for other sites - always hopeful, usually self-assured. Unfortunately, time after time, the result was the same.

With a mounting roster of would-be employers and many polite denials, my chances seemed to be withering.

By now, my friends were placed in good-paying and secure jobs. Frank was off with a major accounting firm in New York City and so was Steve. Jim and Joe had good jobs with the government. Dave worked for IBM and Mike had an executive position all sewed up. I, whose academic record topped theirs, was still out of work. When they wrote or called to find out how and what I was doing, I had nothing to report. I felt so humiliated and useless. They were fending for themselves and contributing to their families. I was still a parasite.

In desperation, I decided to accept almost anything, so I answered an ad specifically seeking handicapped workers. It was a big lump to swallow, but the need to feel self-supporting made me accept it. The job was selling "Eternal Light Bulbs", an overpriced product pitched by pity.

Reluctantly but desperately, I made phone contact with a script that began, "I am handicapped and I am selling Eternal Light Bulbs to support myself."

After hearing myself utter those words, I knew they disgusted me so I simply pitched a few essentials about the product and the price and left it at that. Needless to say, my sales were a disaster, and after three futile days, I turned in my resignation. To me, the job seemed little better than sitting on a street corner with a battered tin cup - the thoughtless music teacher's prediction of long ago.

No accountant. No salesman. No street-corner beggar. There had to be something more I could do. If no employers were willing to give me a chance, I thought it was time to orchestrate my own plans.

To that end, I set up an accounting practice in my home. While I waited for clients, I enrolled in a creative writing course, hoping that some good freelance articles could earn a bit of pocket money. It was the unexpected sale of a few original oil paintings, however, that provided some funds to dabble in stocks. With plenty of time to research and chart the companies that interested me, I quickly turned a nifty profit.

Satisfied that my efforts were finally bearing fruits, I rigidly scheduled my day for maximum results. Rising at six, I wrote for four hours, then read financial newspapers and business periodicals. In the afternoon, I sketched and painted.

Keeping busy helped me shake off the feeling of worthlessness that had almost consumed me, and now, when friends and relatives asked how and what I was doing, I had a few satisfactory answers.

My quest for a "real job" continued and I kept responding to ads. One for a Technical Editor at International Correspondence Schools caught my interest.

Because of past disappointments, I approached this possible

opportunity with trepidation. A tall and dignified middle-aged man conducted the interview in a small office.

After a friendly greeting and a discussion of the job and its qualifications along with totally irrelevant small talk, the ICS representative finally said, "You know, son, sitting across this desk from you with your wheelchair somewhat obscured, I feel like I'm talking with a pretty talented and personable guy. Your attitude and achievements impress me and I would feel privileged to have you a part of our organization."

I could hardly believe my ears. The words sang out like Christmas, New Year and the Fourth of July. Someone believed in me and wanted me at last and that felt very, very good. I had a job at last and a good one.

"When can I start?" I asked eagerly.

The department head smiled. "Tomorrow, if you'd like."

"If I'd like?" I blurted. "I'm ready right now."

We both laughed and mutually agreed that the next day was soon enough.

The job as a Technical Editor was well suited to my skills. It called for me to read galley proofs of raw business manuscripts for content and accuracy, correct errors, and compile questions to accompany the finished product. I enjoyed every aspect of the work except one - its absence of people. I guess "human" interaction was more important than money for me.

Then, luckily, just two months into my ICS work a "people opportunity" came up as if from nowhere. In April of 1968 a second grade teacher at St. Anthony's Grade School unexpectedly left and a replacement was needed immediately. Msgr. Crotti, our parish pastor, offered the position to me.

Though I had often thought about teaching, I believed that my wheelchair might interfere. Despite successful summer work as a playground instructor, I had serious misgivings about a structured classroom. OBVIOUSLY, SAS's Principal shared those same feelings.

"I'll give it a try," the stout nun said with obvious disdain, adding emphatically, "but if it doesn't work out, it doesn't work out."

Unlike the welcoming I had gotten at ICS, I realized I would have to earn Sr. Ann's acceptance and that of the youngsters, too. To our pleasant surprise, our mutual fears proved unfounded. Not long after the second graders said a tearful "Good-bye" to their beloved Miss Sophie, by the very next morning, in fact, they were adoringly in love with their new "Mr. Rinaldi". From my very first moments with them, they redefined my life. I loved their refreshing energy, their unbridled curiosity and their open honesty.

"Mr. Rinaldi, how old are you?"

"Are you married?"

"Mr. Rinaldi, who takes care of you?"

"How do you get dressed?"

"How do you go to the bathroom?"

How? What? When? Where? Why?

All that they legitimately wanted to know. They wanted to know ME - who I REALLY was and that forced me to confront my beliefs, hang-ups and self-deceptions. Through their quest for education, I awesomely understood that these impressionable little characters would be my responsibility, that they would be deeply influenced by me, shaped by my actions and attitudes, tied in to my beliefs and that I could not and would not take that responsibility lightly.

This new role was indeed a point of no return, a defining moment and I eagerly committed myself to it - body, mind and soul, and, in just two short months, I knew this was where I belonged. As a teacher, I had discovered my true niche. My "students" became my "kids". They pumped me up with purpose and my spirit soared.

The most difficult thing I experienced was letting them go. June came and the students went off to unknown places and I returned to college for education courses toward state certification.

In September of 1968, I came back to St. Anthony's and got assigned to teach fifth grade. The thirty-three delightful ten-year-olds provided even deeper enrichment than my previous class. Possibly, because they were older, teacher and pupils formed a productive composite. Together we achieved much more than "book learning" bringing out the best in each other like an atomic chain reaction. My creative imagination blossomed in this stimulating classroom environment and I kept the kids interested through an array of enticing projects.

Soon I was being sought for private tutoring and other academic roles. My schedule grew fuller, but I enjoyed every minute of it. Yet, the challenge to maintain professional objectivity among the students was difficult because a member of my class was my beloved Cousin Donald.

Even before the school year began, I explained that outside of school our relationship was different from what it had to be during school hours. Donald understood and made the adjustment beautifully and though the other youngsters knew that Don and I were first cousins, they soon realized that he did not receive preferential treatment. Don earned his A's in History and he got that deserved D in Math too.

Though I hedged against favoring Don, I was less successful with another student, Angelo Sabatelle. Angelo seemed to be little "Billy Boy" growing up all over again, only this time in a perfectly healthy body. Ang even looked like me at that age. He had the same bright eyes, round, smiling face and ruddy complexion. Our personalities and interests were quite similar, too.

Try as I might, I could not control the deep bond that kept growing between Angelo and myself. Angelo unquestionably realized that he had a special status. He responded in kind but the other youngsters minded little, content that I truly cared about them all.

Our closeness extended way beyond the classroom. Soon my students began paying me visits at home, calling me on the phone and even writing me letters. Boastfully, I must say that they simply could not get enough of their "Mr. Rinaldi".

I humorously even became a part of their sleep, as I discovered when Pamela Pinto disclosed, with a red flush of honest embarrassment, "Mr. Rinaldi, I had a dream about you last night. It was kind of romantic."

The little girl's seriousness made me hide a laugh and I found such joy in so much of what she and her fellow classmates said and did, that my ego often soared. The class was a near perfect outlet for all the love and caring I had to give and I felt almost complete.

Then, in the spring, the euphoric bubble burst when a routine medical checkup and follow-up tests revealed a growth in my mother's uterus. Her doctor suggested surgery but there was no pre-operative certainty that the tumor was either cancerous or benign. I feared the outcome and fervently prayed for her health, her life.

You Can If You Think You Can

On June 3, Mom and Dad celebrated their 25th wedding anniversary and renewed their vows with a special Mass at St. Anthony's. My fifth graders surprised the family by being present for the rite. It was deeply emotional and heart- wrenching.

Mom looked beautiful in a lime green suit and matching pillbox hat, but worry furrowed her brow and distorted her smile. Fear changed my dad's sturdy demeanor too, as he wondered if this might be their last anniversary together.

I worked to mask my own troubled misgivings, looking to the children for courage, strength and hope. This anniversary milestone served up ambivalent emotions - happiness clouded again by the haunting threat of death. Only our collective iron will and bold faith had any chance against it.

As fate would have it, Mom's operation coincided with the last day of school. I reported to work that day to keep myself distracted from my worries, but thoughts about Mom made it impossible to hide the torment. The children instinctively knew that I was in distress.

"Is something the matter?" one student asked with concern.

My quivering voice explained, "My mother's having surgery today and these are difficult moments."

"Then let's pray for her," young Angelo suggested.

In their own simple way, my class added comfort to an otherwise unbearable situation. They offered me the reassurance that God would help and heal.

I shared that with my father and it gave him courage, too.

After supper, Dad returned to the hospital as I waited at home. I spent the tough time alone for the solitude to sort out my thoughts. I loved my mother dearly and life without her seemed unimaginable. I always prayed that I would die first to be spared the agony of life without Mom or Dad. They were my security. They had kept me safe, physically and mentally and I needed them like the air I breathed. Was it selfish to want them to have life as much for my sake as for their own? Would God punish me by taking her away?

Conflicting thoughts toyed with my emotions as I relived images of the past. Incidents when hopes had given way to despair and when despair yielded unexpected hope flashed through my brain and I wondered if maybe this was the way life was supposed to be.

Minutes passed like an eternity as the reflections continued. Finally, Grandpa Beans came with news. The operation was over and a tumor the size of a grapefruit had been removed under a complete hysterectomy. The tumor was benign and Mom was fine and resting comfortably.

Feeling like the heaviest weight had been lifted from my shoulders; I raised my teary eyes to the heavens. With relief and gratitude, I reaffirmed my optimistic spirit and eagerly accepted what tomorrow might bring.

That summer was special, a time of thanks, renewed togetherness, strength, health and healing. With our problems behind us, we took a vacation in upper New York, hoping for a grand good time, but the Catskills escape fell far short of my expectations. The inaccessible sites and an emphasis on the physical made me eager for the week to end. It seriously soured my desire for travel and produced an urge to shape my own recreation.

On the car ride home, I said emphatically, "I've had a lifelong dream for a backyard pool. Who needs the hassles of bad attitudes and barriers? Time to do something creative."

"A pool is no easy undertaking," Mom argued. "I can't handle you alone so you'll be able to get in the water only when your father's around."

Dad added, "Hot summer afternoons looking at the water and waiting to get in might be a tease, Bill. Besides, you're so self-conscious, we'll have to take all kinds of precautions for your privacy."

"Then there's the expense," they stated together.

But the outcome, despite all the negatives, was predictable. Yet again, it was another case of what Billy wanted Billy got. So, the backyard underwent a costly transformation from lawn and landscape to the realization of another great scheme.

As my "Pet Project", the grandiose design of my pool was under my control. Since I never had jewels, cars, and such, why shouldn't I enjoy a little excess? I thought.

The pool was a boon in many ways, some quite surprising. In the water's buoyancy, I rediscovered the joys of self-mobility. It made me able to stand unsupported as I fearlessly shed tubes and life jackets to move about with my own power. How stupendous that sensation made me feel. The consistent exercise improved my general health and strength, too. This free, independent, movement and energy spelled out a bit of "wholeness" that helped me thrive.

The summer of '69 built a sturdier me, in mind and body, and I returned to the classroom in September ready to unleash my increased vitality.

Now assigned to seventh grade, I faced a far different group, adolescents waiting to challenge me far more than the fifth graders ever did. Their raging hormones and teen-age angst called for much more and that became a daily struggle.

By midyear, I finally caught my stride. With imagination, patience and understanding, I gradually won them over. When we found our common ground, everything came together and our achievements mounted. Going beyond the academics, I wrote, produced and staged an original musical comedy for them.

The play, *Mother Goose Revisited*, adapted traditional nursery rhymes into modern social issues. I intended my script to offer sugarcoated lessons for thought and the creative results worked out far better than I could have ever expected.

Like the happy neighborhood shows of my past, I encouraged the multifaceted creative energies of my students and their families. *Mother Goose Revisited* became a community event. With capacity crowds and standing ovations, its popular success opened up many new doors for me, and the principal of Dunmore's parochial high school offered me a job the following September, in a much better paying position.

Success fed upon itself as other high points continued. That summer the acclaimed Hollywood director Martin Ritt slated the filming of *The Molly McGuires* in northeastern Pennsylvania. It was the first major motion picture to be filmed so close to home. I wrote to the noted filmmaker asking to visit the set. My correspondence described my interests as a fan, film reviewer, stockholder in Paramount Pictures and a wanna-be "producer/director". Hardly expecting a response, I was delighted when Mr. Ritt invited me to his location shooting.

My visits to the sets were everything I had imagined. I got to see the technical aspects of film production and was welcomed to hobnob with the cast.

There, at arm's length, were Sean Connery, my James Bond hero, in the flesh and lovely Samantha Eggar, who graciously shared some time with me. Richard Harris actually became a friend. We bonded quickly and often talked about music, movies and other things like longtime buddies. I even brought Richard a record jacket of his hit single *MacArthur's Park* and he excitedly showed it off to his costars.

Funny how life imitates art and these days I had few complaints. This was a magic time with little to edit and a lot to replay--respected teacher, healthy swimmer, stargazer--all such pleasing roles. Spring-board, diving board, never bored. Maybe the best was yet to come.

CHAPTER 12

A New Job

My academic evolution from student to teacher set a pattern for my maturity and growth. In the move from SAS to Dunmore Central Catholic High School, another step in that parallel progression occurred.

DCC was not a large school, just over 500 students, but it differed greatly from old St. Anthony's and those differences sprung from a more complex student body.

Obviously older teens had grittier expectations of their teachers. It wasn't enough to just present the subject matter, confer values and offer gentle guidance. These kids demanded more. They wanted teachers who accommodated their idiosyncrasies, offered a willing ear to their problems, earned their trust and delivered fairness and understanding with every call.

I sincerely tried my best to meet those multiple needs but every day posed another problem. Handling a freshman homeroom, two sections of World Cultures, two of U.S. History, one General Business course and a Senior Religion class, "Human Sexuality and Violence" made fourteen-hour days the norm. Though I felt confident about most of it, my section of forty seniors spelled "trouble" from the start.

How can I hope to teach them anything about "sexuality" and "violence" I wondered? I lacked first hand expertise in both.

A boring textbook didn't help and my students showed their

displeasure by indifference and bad behavior. My overt annoyance only made matters worse. So, teacher/student antagonisms escalated. After months of arduous trying, I finally turned to the Dean for her seasoned advice.

"Give them your patience and your sincerity," she counseled, adding, "and a lot of one-to-one outreach. These kids are crying out for help."

Following her guidance, I altered my approach. I found opportunities to "divide and conquer", making it a point to get to know each one individually while avoiding condescension. Gradually that won them over and by Christmas they were eating out of my hands.

As their respect and trust grew, they came to me with many of their heavy problems and secret thoughts. They talked about many things - alcohol, drugs, sex, parent abuse, failure, guilt, disillusionment, rarely holding anything back.

Why can't I do that, I envied? Why do I bottle up my feelings and hide my fears? Letting them out to a trustworthy someone would surely be better. My dilemma directed me toward the most troubled youngsters and I formed powerful links to them.

One particularly bright junior came to symbolize such empathetic associations. Frank was a young genius and I zealously reinforced his talents and abilities. The straight "A" student painted, wrote poetry, sang, played guitar and he had a large contingent of admiring friends. With such extraordinary potential, he seemed on his way to greatness. Yet, despite all his assets, Frank had a secret addiction to drugs and about midpoint in the school year, he got arrested for possession.

When I heard of the matter, I met privately with the boy hoping to guide him.

"I want to help you, Frank," I opened with a reassuring smile. "Let me."

The teenager dropped his eyes in shame. "If only you could, Mr. Rinaldi. If only you could . . .," he said as tears welled in his eyes.

Seeing the pain, I responded. "I think I know what you might be feeling. I've been there myself - and not so long ago. The drugs, the booze and sex - they called to me, too. I had my thirst for Nirvana."

The boy looked up in disbelief. "Did you - ?"

You Can If You Think You Can

"This chair stood in my way - a blessing, maybe, I guess."

I waited for the words to sink in. Then I went on. "But I've seen far too many who gave in, followed a path of self-destruction. People I've cared about and loved. Maybe that's even more insidious than Muscular Dystrophy, Frank. The horrible waste. Lost family and friends. I don't want you to be among them."

Frank seemed to absorb my words, though, to me, they were hardly adequate. Was I able to provide any comfort, any answers? I wondered.

"Life is precious, Frank. Don't throw it away," I almost begged.

Frank nodded a confirmation. "I'll try, Mr. Rinaldi," he said, "I'll try."

But trying never is enough. This was a turbulent time for Frank, for hundreds of others with heartaches and sufferings, for me. Regardless of energies and intellect, we all seemed to flounder and the disruptive "World Events" of the '60's only made matters worse.

An unpopular war in Vietnam, commercial exploitation of the poor, racial hatred and street violence, environmental deterioration, moral decline and a mistrust of the Establishment transformed the classroom into a forum for debate. The lunacy and chaos of the times demanded that education be made relevant to "LIFE".

I listened to the unrest, the bitterness, the confusions of Frank and so many others and tried to soften their disillusionment. I urged my students to maintain their loyalty to America despite its faults and failures, using every opportunity to state my case.

This zeal labeled me a "flag waver" among some students and when I got wind of their sentiments, I confronted their pride fully.

"I am proud to support my country," I defended. "Despite its shortcomings, it is still the greatest nation on earth."

Truly meaning what I professed, I still feared for those who would soon graduate and go off to who-knows-what. Those concerns motivated me to write a very emotional letter to President Nixon. I explained how difficult it had become, as a country-loving history teacher, to plead the national position on Southeast Asia and I asked him to be more responsive to the youth and to help them feel connected.

I thought that nothing would come of the correspondence but I felt better for having written it. Despite grammatical errors and several misspellings, I sent it off, afraid that a rewrite would let me discard the whole idea.

The next day I told my students that their actions had motivated me to write the Chief Executive and encouraged them to do the same. A week later, on a warm sunny afternoon, I was sitting with my grandparents on the back patio when the phone rang. Grandma Gaetano went inside to answer it. Nonchalantly she extended the phone to me, on its 13-foot cord, out the dining room window.

"Some president wants to talk to you, Bill", she informed.

Calmly I took the phone and answered a normal "Hello".

The caller asked, "Is this Bill Rinaldi of Dunmore, Pennsylvania, speaking?"

I answered in the affirmative.

Then the caller added, "Please hold. The President of the United States would like to speak to you."

It must be Frank or Jim or someone pulling a prank, I thought, deciding to play along with the joke. As the conversation continued, I grew more impressed by the skills of the "Nixon Impersonator" deftly teasing me. Yet "the faker on the other end" was just a bit t-o-o good, and with each word, the picture was changing.

Since the letter was the basis of the call, who else would know its contents this well? Indeed, it had to be the President. My face radiated with shock and excitement. Suddenly Grandma and Grandpa realized what was happening, too, and they could not contain their emotions.

When the conversation ceased, I cradled the phone, shouting and sharing the details of the unbelievable past ten minutes. Grandma excitedly ran to the next door neighbor, who immediately came over for verifications. As if by magic, the news spread and our two city newspapers and a local TV station arrived for an "exclusive".

Seeing the PR possibilities, the White House further hyped the President's outreach and several national press stories and radio and TV interviews kept the excitement alive.

Once again, I became a regional celebrity and the incident had other solid long-range effects, too. For a history teacher, the Kennedy and Nixon connections enhanced my reputation in the classroom and spilled out into the community. It was another significant step forward, and for someone unable to walk at all, the step was monumental. It underscored my own personal sense of dignity and self-worth.

If only all of life's progressions could be so sweet! Life blends the bitter with the sweet and something sudden and catastrophic was just around the corner - again.

Over the years, I had lived through and easily accepted the deaths of five great grandparents. They were old, ill, and ready to pass on to the Eternal Reward. Having known and loved them, I was a fuller person and their presence was sorely missed but it was acceptable, natural.

When Grandpa Rinaldi died, my sorrow flowed from my father and grandmother's grief. That death was somewhat expected and I was prepared.

The remaining members of my immediate family were so close to me that I could not imagine life without them. My parents, Grandma or Grandpa Gaetano, or Grandma Rinaldi made me feel important and secure. They gave me validation, status.

I probably was "Number one" in their lives. Though it may have been egotistical, I frequently questioned them about where I ranked. Having no brothers or sisters, I was clearly #1 on my parents' list. I knew that's where my grandparents placed me, too but I often put them to the test.

"If all your grandchildren were in a burning building, who would you save first?" I'd ask.

"If we were all on a sinking ship . . ."

"If there was only enough serum . . ."

"If just one could, should, would . . ."

"If . . . if . . . if . . .?"

The foolish questions got a variety of responses. Grandma Gaetano's answers were never direct. She would say, "I love all my grandchildren equally, only different. The circumstances of the moment would determine who got saved."

Her evasiveness generally angered me and motivated me to trap her into some commitment.

Grandma Rinaldi told me, "Don't ask such silly questions. What are you, a baby?"

I did not appreciate that either.

Grandpa Gaetano answered with the words I wanted to hear.

"I'd save you, my boy. No doubt about that."

Everyone knew that was true. There was no greater champion, no more forceful defender than Grandpa. If someone hurt his beloved grandson or cut into my happiness, he could really be a tiger.

Grandpa Beans and I were the best of buddies. The closeness that began in infancy strengthened and grew deeper every day and I kept Grandpa young. We played Pinochle together, went to horse races, nightclubs, parties and played off each other's quick wit.

Grandpa was many things to me, a compassionate listener, an understanding sage, a fair mediator, a cautious protector, a willing assistant, a trusted and valued friend and much, much more, always and forever. Or so I hoped.

But, though young at heart, Grandpa was aging. His sparse hair and triangular mustache had gone pure white. His wrinkled skin was splotched with liver spots and his shoulders drooped toward a "spaghetti belly" that stuck out and stretched his buttonholes.

Grandpa seemed determined to combat old age. He ate the foods that kept his body functioning in the way he thought it should. Olive oil, apples, hot peppers and grapefruit became his elixir and two daily jiggers of Canadian Club whiskey "was good for the heart". When his company forced his retirement, Grandpa had more time to pursue other interests so he decided to visit cousins in Florida for a few weeks in the winter of '72.

I hated the separation, but being busy at school helped me get through the two weeks. When Grandpa returned home, he seemed different, more quiet, pensive and glum. Everyone dismissed the mood change as a case of the "mid- winter blahs", but the mood persisted, and Grandpa withdrew even further.

Then, on a fateful Saturday afternoon, Grandpa checked himself into the hospital. On learning the news, Dad, Mom, Grandma and I went directly to the hospital. We found Grandpa looking fine and speaking optimistically.

"I've had blood in my urine for the past several weeks," he disclosed, "but I'm not alarmed. Prostate trouble is quite common for a man of my age."

His calm explanation helped to ease our collective anxieties, but he agreed to call in a specialist for a diagnosis and treatment. The family visited Grandpa daily, turning his hospital stay into a kind of party. In his private room, we literally came with picnic baskets to have supper with him. Though there were times when each of us harbored thoughts of gloom, Grandpa's optimism gave us courage.

A week passed but Grandpa remained in the hospital. Dr. Rosenthal, Dad's long time friend, said nothing about Grandpa coming home. That increased our family's fears and suspicions.

Then, cruelly and unexpectedly, a midnight call awakened us. Mom and I listened intently from the silence of our beds as Dad's one-sided conversation revealed something terribly wrong. When Dad hung up, he told Mom the news.

I strained to hear the words, wanting to know and yet not wanting to know.

"Pop has a tumor on his left kidney. It's almost surely cancerous. The doc says maybe an operation can remove it, but if it's spread to other organs, the prognosis is bad. He only has a slim chance."

The revelation made Mom cry. Alone in the dark of his room, I experienced no tears. I experienced terror.

No! Not Grandpa! My Grandpa wanted to live so much and he did it so beautifully. He deserved more. His life made others happier, fuller. All that would be gone without him. I just couldn't take that. It was simply too much.

No one slept that night. The possibility of losing Grandpa was almost unbearable. Yet, we had to get through this, one way or another. We needed all the collective strength we could muster.

In the morning, Dad discussed a plan with us. Grandma and Grandpa had to be spared the awful diagnosis. Grandma, so innocently naive, might be easy to fool, but how could we deceive Grandpa? He deserved our honesty and respect more than anyone did. Did we have an obligation or the right to hide him from the truth?

Debating the question was like playing God but this "leading role" no one really wanted to play.

When we visited Grandpa that afternoon, the artificial quality of the situation seemed so surreal. Gramps was propped up on a pillow, looking smaller, farther away. We babbled about trifles, but I knew our words could not disguise the truth in our eyes. He was not deceived. Each succeeding visit saw Grandpa diminishing, slipping further and further away. The day before his surgery, everyone attempted to be optimistic and casual. It was a time to laugh and joke and love, to flaunt joy in the face of "that haunting grim reaper". He had no place here. As the hour grew late, Dad made the first move to leave but Grandpa asked for a little more time.

A little more time! A forever!

Finally, the moment of departure had to be faced. Grandma, Mom and Dad agreed to return the following morning, but for me, this was "good-bye." Dad wheeled me to the side of Grandpa's bed. Our hands linked. The touch was intense. It symbolized our bond. When our hands parted, that was a symbol, too. The broken touch seemed so final to me, to us both, and I sensed that this was our last living moment together.

I suppressed my tears. "Good-bye, Gramps," I sputtered.

Grandpa simply said, "Good-bye."

Dad turned me away and took me from the room, trying desperately to hide his own tear stained face. These moments, that touch, those tears, would be remembered always.

Tuesday's surgery was an ordeal, lasting over five hours. Now a waiting game had to be played. Grandpa went from surgery to the recovery room to intensive care. When he gained consciousness, our family was permitted to visit him for three minutes, four times daily. One person at a time went in and everyone except me got some precious time with him. He asked about me to each, telling them of a dream that he had about me.

"How I wish I could see him again," he whispered weakly.

Grandpa's wish was not to come true. That night Dr. Rosenthal told us that so many of his organs had been affected that everyone should prepare for the worst. It was only then that Mom told Grandma what we had known all along.

On Saturday, my parent's 27th wedding anniversary, Grandpa rallied. He ate some Jell-O and had energy to talk to them. However, at 6:00 a.m. Sunday, the phone rang with news that Grandpa was critical. The family rushed to him. I waited at home with my cousin Patti. Each hour we called for a report.

"No change."

Minutes passed like a tortured eternity. Ominously the day went from sunshine to rain. Patti and I tried to find ways to pass the agonizing wait. Then I saw them. First Mom and she were crying, then Dad, looking lost, finally Grandma, so helpless and now so alone.

Grandpa was gone.

In that second, I knew my deepest grief. It was so crushing, so painful and complete. If only my legs could help me escape, even briefly, for a moment of private release. I was trapped. I couldn't allow myself to cry, not in front of them. They needed my strength. With a courage that surprised me, I found words that soothed Grandma, Mom, everyone. Then I asked for that moment alone, to pray and sort out my thoughts.

Dad brought me to my bedroom and left, closing the door to create the sanctuary I needed so desperately. It was O.K. now to be weak. I cried, sobbed, heaved anguish, grateful that these were my tears alone.

Cousin Annie came to get me several minutes later. She threw her arms around my shoulders and felt me trembling. She knew, as they all did, how much I had lost.

A part of me, that part that loved life, people and joyousness was gone. I was empty. Numb.

Was loving someone so much really worth the pain of this torturous loss?

In that moment, my only defense was to turn inward, to harden my shell and keep a safe distance. I can't let myself love like this again because, if I do, then I am going to hurt, hurt so badly it might destroy me.

In this horrible tragedy, a damaging change was taking place. The once zestful, happy lover of life had given himself up to cynicism. And, in a newly found, safer world without emotions, survival assumed different tones. Hate, despair, self-pity took over and my spirit went into a tailspin.

Muscular Dystrophy hadn't killed me. Cruel pragmatists and forceful pessimists didn't destroy my will. But the death of my beloved grandfather undid it all. I still prized life, if only to cling to it because Grandpa had treasured it so intently, but life had narrowed its focus.

Bill, the man, wanted to be a child again, cuddled safely in the fetal position, content with self-love, gratification and satisfied with a simplistic peace. That whole world of "others" held too much risk. Caring, sharing, and pairing were threats to life itself.

Grandpa, you're gone! Can I, should I still love you? Can you, will you still love me? What is dying like? Does it hurt as badly as losing you? If you love others and they are taken away, then you must die many times. What could be worse?

The primal searching, the unanswered questions returned again.

How many more times would they continue to haunt me? In the bitter pain that I was feeling, I could fathom nothing harsher. For me such reasoning marked an end, an end unlike any other.

CHAPTER 13

When One Door Closes...

Once upon a time, there was this cute little baby boy. He had the right stuff from which greatness might be expected. He was a healthy, bright, white, middle class, American male and his potential seemed boundless. With such ingredients for success, maybe the lad could even grow up to become President of the United States.

Somehow, the tiny infant developed differently than other children. Expectations and attitudes changed as harsh realities darkened the possibilities.

If the doctors and medical experts were correct, the child "wasn't going to live very long", and the grand fairy tale of exciting hopes and glorious dreams would not end happily ever after. Instead decline, disease, degeneration, devaluation and desperation would ravage him and bring a tragic closure to his story.

So distressing was the saga that the boy's parents masked his vulnerability and created a protective bubble to guard him. They molded him to cherish life and believe wholeheartedly in his personal worth and dignity. Thus, the child forged ahead determined to make the best of his physical shortcomings. Through intellect, imagination and will, he blossomed and grew, building an impressive list of accomplishments along the way.

Wanting neither pity nor help, the boy projected an image of self-sufficiency, and with the help of his parents and grandparents, he was able to maintain the charade. The illnesses, declines and death of his defense squad shook his confidence and he timidly withdrew into himself, laboring over how he would survive in their absence.

His parents shared those same fears, but his mother, true to her religious convictions, was confident that God would somehow provide. His father, on the other hand, was not so sure. Seasoned by suspicions and mistrust, he became the "Mighty Protector". Only he could assist and guide his son. From infancy through many sleepless nights, he was and would be there to meet every need, automatically and without question.

The dedication took its toll and the steady diet of disappointments and despair brought the "Mighty Protector" to his knees. That was the Rinaldi family saga, the script of generations. Now things took another twist. Until Grandpa died on me, I was basically willing to play the family's "Glad Game", being a Disney-perfect Pollyanna. But now, the fairy tale was over - at least for me.

For eighteen months, I turned away from people, participating only on the periphery. Mom and Dad surely saw my gloom but compensated by pumping their efforts to la di da life.

In that regard, Christmas of 1973 was no different. Even they got their grim wake-up call that holiday. At a post-Christmas dinner, the festivities fumbled when Dad doubled up with severe stomach pains. He rushed off to the bathroom and emerged several minutes later, visibly quivering and ashen.

"I'm not feeling very well," Dad announced. "Will you excuse me?"

"What's the matter?" Mom questioned with concern.

Dad responded evasively," I went to the bathroom and eliminated a substantial amount of blood."

It wasn't so much what he said as how he said it that sounded an alarm. Mom hardly hesitated, "I'm calling the Doctor - now," she said.

Dr. Demko heard her concerns and urged that Dad be taken to the Hospital Emergency Room immediately. After a fearful process of investigation and analysis, Dr. Demko revealed the bad news. Dad had colon-rectal cancer and he needed an operation F-A-S-T.

The diagnosis brought back other painful moments, Mom's tumor and operation in '69 and Grandpa's death in '72. Now Dad faced the issue of mortality. Another key player was going down. How might this family survive yet another life-or-death crisis? I wondered. The test would come soon enough.

As Dad awaited surgery, our problems mounted. Mom struggled with a dual barrage of duties. My twenty-four hour cycle of needs and Dad's simultaneous dependence placed a heavy burden on her. I realized that she could not handle the expanded difficulties indefinitely. Without Dad's help, what's left for me? I wondered. Humiliation? Exposure? More limits? Hell!

If that was my fate, then why should I continue my struggle to live? My only freedom seemed to be in death, my death. So, this marked a time to get on with it.

With that as my unstated mission, I refused medication for an ordinary winter flu as my fevers soared. I gave in to the thickening phlegm and a hacking cough that weakened me further.

My plan for self-annihilation was proceeding perfectly. Ravaged by my mental and physical state, hallucinations of the Christmas decorations, tree, tinsel, lights and presents mockingly glared at me through memories of far better days. In my despair, I pondered the New Year with trepidation. What should I resolve in the "wake" of another year's terror? Clearly, my fight was gone. I had given up and turned myself over to God.

But others were not as willing to let me slip away. Friends and family, who had been at my side through the best and worst of times, made it their mission to get me back on track. Chief among them was my college buddy, Mike.

"I'm not going to let you throw in the sponge," Mike said with conviction. "There's plenty of people who care about you and want to help . . . if you'll let them."

"He's too proud for that," Mom countered.

Without a moment's hesitation, Mike came back even more forcefully. "Get over it, Bill. Your pride won't stand in my way and I won't let it stand in yours either. Don't you trust me? Isn't the value of our friendship deep enough yet?"

The words gave me food for thought and I mulled them over and over again. Could any human being get me past my father's illness and attitude, my mother's desperation and failing strength and my own defeated desperation? Or was I truly alone?

The answer came quite unexpectedly with a saving visit from my sixteen-year-old cousin, Greg. Like Mike, Greg had a mission - to bring me back to what I was - the man who took joy from life. Like Mike, Greg did not mince words.

"We've been drifting apart for the past few years," he opened, "and now you need me and I still need you, too."

I was taken off guard. I understood half of my young cousin's remarks. I had indeed stepped aside as Greg's teacher, mentor and substitute father. Time and circumstances had altered those roles. But flip-flopping "helper" and "helped" seemed inappropriate and unfair. It was too much for a carefree teenager to bear.

"You don't understand Greg," I argued. "My care requires a lot, more than you should handle. It's simply not fair to you."

Greg saw it differently. "It's what I want to do and I know I can. Please trust me."

Though I was moved by Greg's sincerity, I held steadfast. "Greg, you have no idea how much help I really need. I can't put that burden on you."

"I have no idea? That's where you're wrong," he challenged as he turned me to face him. "I've known you all my life and the struggle you face every day. Don't push me aside. Lean on me. Don't let me feel I've failed even before you've given me a try."

The student/teacher challenge struck the right chord. Greg deserved some sensible response. Yet, I drew a blank.

"There are no tests for this, Greg," I said. "We're not talking Algebra or Current Events here."

Greg did not hesitate. "But there are other ways I can prove myself. Let me take you to the bathroom."

The words hit like another shock. Something so private and long guarded was my parents' exclusive domain, a sanctum. How could I give in to this?

My stupefied silence provoked Greg further.

"What's the big deal, Bill? Everybody pees, you know. That's mighty natural. Or do you have something I don't?"

His deliberate nonchalance put a different spin on things and I was more embarrassed by my own backward sheepishness, than by the physical aspects of the process. Greg had cornered me successfully, so I reluctantly agreed.

"Well, OK. If you really want to and think you can, let's give it a try."

Greg ushered me into the bathroom and competently got down to business. It was all so simple, so easy.

With a free-flowing stream of urine and one flush of the toilet, decades of pressures and hang-ups went down the drain and the relief felt simply wonderful.

Greg's demeanor clearly reflected his pride. "See," he noted. "Success. I told you I could do it. So what's next?"

"What's next?" Indeed.

In one brief but liberating moment, things were altered forever. The entangling chains slipped away and the cautions, excuses, half-truths, cover-ups, schemes, plots and secret devices were gone at last. I was free.

Greg had given me a most precious gift. He had restored my will to live, and much, much more. His warm, caring ways salvaged my dignity and I learned that honest, open outreach would not destroy me or compromise my self worth. Weak muscles, useless legs, barely functional arms and a misshapen body made me no less a man. Good people would accept me as a total being, the whole bigger and better than the sum of its imperfect parts. There were no more reasons to hide.

With Greg's help, I had found a means to survive the crisis.

Thankfully, my metamorphosis was contagious. Mom was also greatly relieved by her son's improvement and the assistance she received from Greg. Dad, too, was comforted by the household news. The invincible Rinaldis were back in the fight.

Stimulated by the fast-developing events in our lives, Mom shared a perplexing dream with me. "Grandpa came to visit me at a small house by the ocean. He had a broad, beaming smile. What do you think it means?"

I thought for a while then responded, "Two possibilities. Either

Dad will pull through and get well or he will be joining Grandpa in heaven. Whatever might occur is in God's hands."

"I guess we have to accept His Will. Tomorrow is New Year's Eve. Bill, pray with me for Dad - and us."

Almost simultaneously, the phone rang. It was Dad and his tone spoke volumes.

"I want to conquer this cancer and come home to my family," he promised.

That resolve was the spirit we had longed for and we radiated with optimism. The Rinaldis were ready to face January 1. On the day of Dad's surgery, Mom went off to the hospital in the early morning. Her sisters-in-law and my grandmothers accompanied her. Aunt Kate stayed home with me.

At either end, the slow passage of time grew into an endurance contest of expressed and unexpressed emotions as each of us wondered who would crack first, of what fate might have in store. We tried to support and comfort one another as the tension mounted but anxieties soared.

Despite my fears, I believed that powerful positive forces were at work to make for happy results, but Grandma Rinaldi was in a far different frame of mind. She was an anguished mother whose son teetered between life and death and she hardly knew what to say or do. Frantic and confused, she voiced a pact with God.

"If a life can be traded for a life," she bargained, "I will give mine up so that Alex can be spared."

I was moved by her plea and tried to comfort her but nothing I did or said eased her broken heart. How difficult this must be for a mother, I thought.

My grandmother's plight helped me understand what my own mother must have felt for so many years. She was a rock, an inspiration and I admired her as never before. Now I had to be equally strong while every second continued to test me.

Mom called around ten. "Dad's surgery has started," she informed us. There was no further word throughout the morning.

Then, around two, she called again. "The surgeon said the procedure went well. The cancer has been removed and Dad will recover but he'll have a permanent colonostomy."

If this was a bad news/good news dilemma, it was better than what I had bargained for and I thanked God for another miracle. Our tears were of joy rather than sorrow and it seemed truly a time for celebration.

Again, my euphoria was short-lived. At supper Dr. Demko called, to tell me what I might expect in the days and weeks to come.

"Your dad may have made it through the surgery all right," he opened, "but brace yourself for what lies ahead."

I hardly understood the doctor's meaning.

"Colonostomies change people, Bill," the physician continued. "Your dad won't be as he was, particularly psychologically. He's going to need you now more than ever. You have to be subtle in order to make him still feel needed, useful and important. Don't let him down."

Surely, Dr. Demko was prophetic. The next six months presented a challenge of readjustments far greater than any that I had anticipated. Everyone had changed and the altered personalities cried out for a new identification.

Tested and strained by the differences, Dad and I suffered from even greater estrangement.

As his body healed, Dad tried to regain control, but I refused to relinquish my recently acquired liberties. Greg had stepped in to many of the tasks and responsibilities that had once been Dad's and I liked it that way. My cousin's unconditional cooperation opened doors and I wanted to explore what lay beyond.

Almost like a teenage peer, I made Greg my inseparable aide, friend, student, brother, even "Baby Papa!", a term of endearment we both understood. Greg had become my arms and legs, tolerant and accepting of my ideas and actions and now I had a soul mate again.

But in our closeness, my parents felt shut out and a rivalry began in earnest. They viewed Greg as a threat and they harbored a subtle hostility toward the fourth party now living under their roof. They were ill-prepared for his active, healthy teen-age energies, his messy midnight showers, clothes not hung up, long hair, gargantuan appetite, poor table etiquette and his host of frenzied friends. These might have all been overlooked if I had not championed his actions with such zealous permissiveness. Acting out of spite, I encouraged Greg's less admirable traits, while flaunting my own newly found freedoms. Like an uncaged beast, I went out in all kinds of weather, kept late hours and disclosed little about where I went and what I was doing. Putting my parents' feelings last, I tried out my wings with little or no thought about their worries.

Stubbornness prevailed as antagonisms swelled and though I was mostly at fault, Greg was an easier target. Therefore, my parents laid their anger on him.

As Dad's strength increased, our battles and resentments built, and I feared Greg would leave. Yet, the only path to preserving my freedom - to a life of my own - to Bill being Bill - was holding my ground.

CHAPTER 14

Coming Into My Own

The kind hand of God plus good fortune, ideal timing, perseverance and the intervention of caring helpers allowed for my survival and metamorphosis into a man.

Like the Phoenix rising from the ashes, after Dad's serious illness, his "Billy Boy" gave way to a newly reincarnated being, a man with an identity all his own. At long last, I was separate, independent. I was master of my own fate and fully responsible for all that I might be. No longer constricted, I finally laid claim to my rightful place.

Thus far, I've told you about "him", this "Billy Boy". Now it's time to tell you about ME!

Like everyone else, I am a product of genes, environments and unique experiences, the complex blend of nature and nurture. In that, we share a common ground. But to understand myself more, revisiting my past has altered my perspective. The embryo, the infant, the child, the teen, the novice on his way to adulthood seems like the stages of long ago. They are the fading bits of yesterday, that travel with me through today, on my journey toward tomorrow.

In our inter-dependent Universe where many people play significant roles in the development of others, surely our parents are primary players.

Fortunately for me, mine were very special. My mom and dad conceived me in love and remained committed to my well being through the span of their unselfish lives. Since my body required baby-like nurturing and protection, they unwittingly kept me their perpetual child. How hard they tried to shield me from grown-up stings. Their behavior left my adolescent curiosities and appetites unfulfilled. When Greg set me free, I became captain of my own ship, setting its course for the unknown islands of my desires.

Overripe, I was almost bursting. With reckless abandon, I made bold plans to revisit the vices from my past, push the envelope further and explore new terrain. Curiosity mixed with defiance as I set out to tackle my INDEPENDENCE, to toast the future, to get very "stinkin" drunk.

With that as a goal and feeling no need to hide the thirst, I orchestrated a boozing binge. Slugging ten shots of Seagram 7, one right after another, I sent my senses reeling. The raw alcohol just about did me in and with unleashed inhibitions, I ranted a litany of suppressed obscenities in a foul-mouthed barrage.

My friends found my antics quite amusing and the insanely inebriated me did too. With the morning, however, double vision, a pounding head, nausea and queasiness made for a grimmer reality.

When Mom served me breakfast, I barely had time to ask for a basin before the night's hedonistic intake gushed from me. But vomiting was part of the release and I hurled with pride. My parents asked what had caused the uncharacteristic "tummy dumper" and undigested pepperoni pizza got the blame.

This began the series of lies, which accompanied my new freedoms, because I still wanted to seem innocent and pure to them.

I guess these were dishonest times for my generation and me. The conflicting values of the '60's and '70's have fueled our confusions. Vietnam, Woodstock, free love and drugs prompted us toward irresponsibility and deceit. I spun my wheels with much the same frenzy of conflict and rebellion. Nothing and everything seemed wrong and permissive experimentation marked the climate of these troubled times.

Alcohol had been the drug of choice during my college years and though marijuana and LSD were available, most of my circle shied away from them. I had my curiosities but I stayed drug free, too.

You Can If You Think You Can

I had changed, got caught up in a search for "highs" and psychedelic dimensions beyond the limits of my "wheelchair-bound" body. So I tried smoking a joint at a "divorce" party after most of the guests were gone.

It was another secret act, again neither fun nor fulfilling and it took me to the dumb, dark things that belong to the realm of irresponsible idiots. I was embarrassed by my actions, but my friends accepted my bad behavior as I came to grips with my own stupidity.

Booze? Not a happy experience.

Drugs? Even worse.

Sex? Hmmm! Now, what about that?

From the days of my youth, good old-fashioned lust had never stopped boiling inside me. Childhood experimentation, books, movies and conversations with those who indulged reinforced the appeal.

How can you "get laid" (to quote the popular vernacular) when you have no self-mobility to get into the position, I wondered. And how and where do you find a willing partner with the understanding to meet this need? I thought such experiences would be impossible for me, but thank God, I was wrong.

Some of my friends knew my desire and one of them put me in touch with a young woman, who "discretely serviced", a limited number of men. To call her a "prostitute" would do her a great injustice. She was the first woman I came to know, in the Biblical sense, and she was wonderful. . kind, beautiful and understanding.

Sadie guided me through that crucial rite of passage with tenderness and joy. She showed me that sex could be a gentle, giving act, devoid of shame or sin. Sadie's subtle manner set that simple male instinct free and helped me find mental peace in physical relief.

Though my "first" time was awkward, intimate and unique, it was a comedy/drama of spectacular proportions. For very practical reasons, I needed a cooperative "third party", an understanding friend, to get me a room and help me into bed. Discretely he left us alone when those deeds were done and Sadie took care of the rest.

For a while we just talked. Then she touched so I could touch, too. There were actions, reactions, and a very contented smile. It seemed very natural to have her beside me, to feel her body pressed against mine and my release was pleasant, enlightening and peaceful.

It made me feel every inch a man and I will love her always for the completeness she gave me.

In our man/woman intimacy, I explored many things and though we spent several more evenings' together, lust was never a part of it. Lust, for me, was much baser - an impersonal exploitation of user and used. Though I saw its perverseness, I had to try a bit of that, too.

When opportunity knocked (twice), I seized it. During a midwinter trip to Las Vegas, the surreal allure of the city's high-paced life style, neon palaces, fancy casinos, glitzy feathered and jeweled showgirls completely dazzled me.

Here anything could be yours if you "flashed the cash" and my companion and I were amazed at the "escort services" blatantly promoted in the phone book and street flyers.

The going rates were far too expensive for our budget but the sleazy life off the strip was something we wanted to explore. We separated from my parents and other traveling companions to take in a burlesque show where the main attraction was Flaming Amy, a fire-eating Amazon who performed incredible feats of strength and acrobatics.

As part of her act, Amy came into the audience to tease and entice the crowd and I was among the men she goaded into eating fire. When she returned to the stage, she had watches and wallets to highlight her pick-pocketing gimmick. Everyone laughed and applauded her skills and we left the theater completely entertained.

It was very late and my friend and I were ready to go back to our hotel for a good night's sleep. As he wheeled me back, a young black girl approached us.

"Wanna party?" she asked.

Reflexively, I inquired, "How much?"

She then proceeded to give us quotations like a stockbroker, offering adventures I had never heard of before. The opportunity seemed just too fantastic to pass up and I found myself negotiating the deal of a lifetime.

"Meet us in the lobby of the Frontier at 3:00 a.m.," I told her, quite doubtful that she would show up.

There she was - primped and prompt. So, for a few affordable hours, we coupled and cuddled in my room - just four rooms down the hall from my unsuspecting parents.

With such risk and glitz, the caper unfolded more like a James Bond adventure than a sexy escapade in neon Nevada and it was the only successful score I made there. Pants down and pockets empty, Vegas gave new meaning to an unforgettable trip and I salute our travel agent for the sights and surprises.

But topping even that, the ultimate raunchy experience of my lifetime was a wild afternoon on New York's infamous 42nd Street. The Big Apple with its towering skyscrapers and lavish Broadway plays held deep fascination for me ever since I was two. Though the Cornell Medical Center was uppermost on the agenda back then, we continued to make a few trips every year purely for pleasure.

On one of those excursions, my friend Joe and I headed for the mega-sleazy district off 8th Avenue. We began our itinerary in The Metropol, a topless-bottomless bar. Six dollars a beer and a tip in the naked dancer's shoe was hardly cost effective entertainment so off we went to a triple-X movie theater's bargain matinee.

The small, smelly cinema was dark and dingy and my wheelchair barely fit in the narrow aisle. We had just started to watch the explicit on-screen perversions when two beautiful young girls came behind us and whispered offers in our ears.

"There are massages available in the basement for $10," one girl bartered.

"Steps?" Joe asked on my behalf.

"Yea," she nodded. "Afraid so."

"Too dangerous for me," I remarked.

"It will be worth it," the other woman promised.

Since I had no intention of risking the danger, I turned her down, but my friend accepted her offer. So, there I was, alone, in a porn house on 42nd Street. Who'd a thunk it? Who'd believe it? I could hardly believe it myself. This certainly was the ultimate Everest for me.

Yet the summit had hardly been reached. There was more. Some ten minutes later, Joe returned in thorough disgust. He boisterously complained, "I've been royally ripped," he balked. "It cost me $40 for a bare minimum of sweet nothings. Let's leave this joint pronto."

A young lady overheard Joe's angry words. "Let me do you better," she peddled. Looking directly at me, she said, "More for less."

"But I can't get to the basement," I lamented.

She pointed. "The projection room, cozy and private."

What more could I want? So off I went, for whatever she might have in mind. Letting her lead, I found myself encouraged to act as she directed. With uninhibited eagerness, I hardly thought about the circumstances and her exuberant pleasure-giving set up a passionate tidal wave of Titanic fury. Yet just when my She-Captain was raising the sail, the film broke. Completely unflappable, the girl continued, never to sway from her skillful maneuvers. As the machine whirred noisily, a projectionist re-entered the room. He matter-of-factly did his repairs without skipping a beat, acting as if I wasn't even there.

The whole situation was too ridiculous to be embarrassing. I could hardly believe its sordid, silly wantonness, but it counted as a conquest of epic dimensions.

The alcohol, drugs and sexcapades had a necessary place. My wild adventures, curiosities and fantasies had become realities across three time zones from Vegas to NYC and I felt downright triumphant. By accomplishing these daring deeds, my feelings of denial, inadequacy, and inferiority ended. I would not die an unwilling "virgin" after all. I was finally aware that some of my systems and some of my strengths were as good as anyone else's.

Thus, I learned that manhood and maturity are not body-based. They rightfully exist in the MIND and SPIRIT and these were operating just absolutely fine.

CHAPTER 15

The Visitor

It seems that every major shift in life triggers a chain reaction. Thus, when I unleashed irrevocable forces of self-determination, discovering my purpose, the "Why" of my being, became an even more compelling quest. With some fresh, new opportunities for personal growth, my knowledge of who I was continued to explode.

But such cosmic investigations produced questions whose answers often eluded me.

Seeking clarifications, I looked for experts, gurus from the present and past to reveal what they could. I ravenously devoured the classic books and films and longed for stimulating people, places and things to inspire me. The thirst propelled me toward many meetings of the minds and my classroom was a natural arena for that. My idealistic young students challenged me to explore a panorama of ideas, to digest and evaluate them and deduce valid conclusions for their well-being as well as my own. The students motivated me to stay current and relevant, to keep the door open for any point of view.

In my enthusiasm, I welcomed a colorful parade of "guests" into my life. That horrified the ultra-conservative school administration. The principal frequently warned me to narrow my outreach and I sometimes came dangerously close to getting the ax. Despite the restraints, I held on tightly to my unorthodox ways.

"You're risking your career," my dad cautioned.

"This is my career," I defended.

Censorship, criticisms, practical imperatives only made me bolder and I flung them aside in support of free thought. For too many years, I had been ghettoized in an environment where strangers threatened, where actions were neatly boxed, where conformity was the only option. As an educator, I couldn't let my students succumb to that.

But such behavior made my role more difficult and I needed supportive allies. After a time, I found the Association for Research and Enlightenment. The A.R.E. focused on the metaphysical and at our weekly meetings we discussed the ideas of Socrates, Plato, Aristotle, Thomas Aquinas and recognized Twentieth-Century scholars. With Edgar Cayce's *Search for God* books as a guide for meditation and yoga, we dutifully explored the power of positive thinking, self-awareness, telepathy, clairvoyance, psychokinesis, Silva mind control, psychic healing, numerology, astrology and other abstract beliefs.

By becoming more open to these ideas and more, I reconnected with God. Spirituality and soul seeking put a different spin on things for me. Material values paled as I sought better and bolder ways to contribute to the family of man.

One means of doing this was the sponsorship of a Vietnamese refugee.

As a World Cultures and Social Studies teacher, interest in the global community beckoned to me. Dr. Tom Dooley was one of my heroes and his books about the social and political situation in Southeast Asia bothered and frustrated my sensibilities, but I was at a loss to do something about it

When Saigon fell in 1975, two of my close friends provided homes for several displaced Vietnamese families. That lit a spark. Possibly sponsoring a refugee could finally assuage me.

I presented the idea to my parents, but they expressed very legitimate concerns about the undertaking. Yet I persisted. I had grand visions of what I might achieve. As a patriotic American, I saw favorable prospects of integrating a needy "DP" into my classroom, my household and my life. In a very symbiotic way, my students could tutor him in our language and customs and he could share his experiences and heritage with them. If we provided a place in our home, Mom and Dad could get some help and respite with my care. As for me, I'd have done Tom Dooley proud.

Theoretically, the plan seemed flawless. Overcoming their misgivings, my family rearranged our household to accommodate our "Vietnamese guest".

I eagerly awaited word on the identity of the unknown stranger soon to be living under our roof. Like an expectant father, I was excited but a little scared about the responsibility and its impact on the key players.

After a very short time, the Bureau of Catholic Services called to announce the details of whom, what and when.

"Your DP's name is Tran van Than. He's twenty-three, in good health and speaks very little English. He'll be arriving by Martz Bus at 3:30 on Thursday. "

The arrival came much quicker than we expected, a mere 48 hours of official notification. Then, on September 30, 1975, Mom, Dad, Grandma and I went to the bus station to meet our new houseguest.

Than was unmistakable in the crowd getting off the bus, a small, dark, obviously Oriental man with a very desperate look. His ragged clothing hinted of his lack of preparedness too. Sporting just a light jacket, baggy jeans and open sandals, he was probably shaking as much from his apprehensions as from the autumn chill. All Than carried was a duffel bag, which he clenched tightly.

Dad shook Than's hand. Mom hugged him warmly. Grandma and I approached him with encouraging smiles, hoping that our body language would reassure him.

Thank God, our gestures were understood.

"I, Than," the young foreigner opened. "I speak only Vietnamese and a little French. Sorry."

It was an awkward start and the ten-minute ride home seemed almost an eternity. Much was needed to be said without any words to say it.

I really don't know how we ever got past the first week, but Than was very bright, eager to learn and generous to help. We felt an instant affinity toward him and he nestled into our routine easier than I might have imagined.

Each day, I would take him to school where members of the honor society taught him our language and rudimentary skills for cultural adjustments. After school, he would retreat to his quarters and study until supper.

We ate together and used the opportunity to synthesize our languages and our customs. Than assisted Mom and Grandma with the cleanup and then he and I would take another hour to work on his English.

Later, he would retire to his four rooms (our former playroom and furnished basement), where he would have the quiet and privacy to study and deal with his thoughts. He made good use of the tape recorder and small TV I gave him and he seemed grateful for any kindness.

We took Than almost everywhere we went, introduced him to our friends, and guided him through several "first time" situations. In less than a month, he was able to communicate quite well. The social worker, assigned to his case, was extremely impressed by his progress and we felt quite proud about what we had achieved.

As language skills improved, Than shared much of his life with me, though he was far less open to others. He was very friendly, but he maintained a guarded posture and an unassertive carefulness. The only exception to his cautious interactions was Grandma. Than loved "Mommie" as he called her and they made an adorable twosome. It was a joy to watch them together. He looked after her gently and she gave him a unique kind of love.

I learned much from Than as days passed into weeks, then months. He was born to privilege, the eldest son. Besides conventional schooling, his training included the "teachings of the mountain savages". Than also had extraordinary manual dexterity and mechanical savvy. His martial arts skills and music talents made him capable of many things and he had several optimistic aspirations.

Yet horrifying tales of his homeland provided a stimulating perspective for cross-cultural comparisons, contrasts and what he shared was good for us both.

As Than adjusted to America, our family and friends encouraged him and offered him financial help.

We found him a variety of jobs. At Christmas, he received over a hundred gifts and everything seemed to be wonderfully in synch. Then an unusual event changed the daily harmony.

Before the New Year (1976), an area college held a party for the regional refugees and their sponsors. The college presented a lavish feast, a moving drama, ethnic music and a fine atmosphere for socializing. Than attended in his finest new clothes. I thought this would be a happy occasion for him, but as he spoke to his people in their native tongue, his demeanor went from frivolity to sadness.

The next day I asked him about it. "Did you have a nice time? You appeared somewhat disturbed."

"A little," he answered evasively.

I saw a need to pursue the matter further. "Please tell me more," I gently prodded.

He offered an explanation. "Many Vietnams treat poor here. Bad sponsors and violent. We not slaves. My people feel betrayed. They have nowhere to go."

I sensed his anger. Defensively I inquired, "Do you feel that way, too?"

"You good to me - too good to me," he said.

Shortly after that conversation Than changed noticeably. He began spending less time with us and more time with the regional refugees. He stopped coming to school, avoided chores around the house, left his belongings scattered about and displayed a markedly antagonistic attitude. He quit his job, abused his household privileges, and was taking license to party with questionable friends.

Than's actions really irritated my father, who began to chastise and reprimand him. Things got worse when his tougher-looking companions began helping themselves to the whiskey in our liquor cabinet. Though never rowdy, they kept late hours in the basement beneath us as we slept. In the mornings, as Dad and I braved the cold winter to go to work, Than remained in bed. All his ambition and drive seemed to be gone and even beloved "Mommie" got curt replies and harsh rejection from him. However, Than maintained his respect for me. Though I rarely corrected him, he followed my direction and advice to the letter.

Four beautiful months gave way to two unexplainably difficult ones. Then one Tuesday, Mom picked me up at school and she was crying. I couldn't imagine what had happened.

She explained in exasperation, "I heard Than rummaging about late in the morning and when I offered him breakfast, he did not answer. I looked down the steps and saw him seated on the couch with a suitcase at his side. When I questioned him further, he told me he could not explain. He says he would tell you."

Frankly, I was relieved by what she said because it hinted of the end of a relationship that now caused strain to all of us. When I came home, Than sheepishly approached me. He obviously was searching for the right words.

"Bill," he began, "I must leave. I am failing in my attempts to be a man, an American man. You are too good to me. I do not try."

I wish I could reproduce the ensuing conversation exactly. It revealed so much. Than said that the love and care we offered diminished his desire to make a life for himself. To be a man, he had to make it on his own.

I, maybe more than my family, understood. Of course, there were some unsaid things and I'm sure we both felt disappointed that our over-inflated expectations had come to this.

"Than," I began, "you are free to leave us if that's what you want."

He bowed his head and remained thoughtfully silent for a long while. Finally, he said, "May I visit you as a friend?"

"Our door will remain open Than and I wish you the best."

Than moved out that evening, first to live in the area with other Vietnamese, then to Illinois where he became a sewing machine repairman. We saw him several times after his move, then never again. I often wonder what has become of him. I would like to believe that we set some sound footing for him to build his American life. Yet, whatever we may have done for Than, he certainly made an indelible impact on me. He taught me to appreciate my country more than ever, to respect our freedom and general security and to value the struggle for independence and the merits of interdependence.

How much we take for granted! How much we need to know!

For most Americans, good things may come too easily and we may act as if we are entitled. Sometimes it takes extraordinary occurrences to bring those notions home.

Through prayer groups, people like Than and that whole range of opportunities from which profound meanings flow, I found out more about my complex self and my equally complex world. Such mental exercises fueled a surging appetite within me to go forward and do and do and do—and all these opportunities were gratefully welcome.

CHAPTER 16

The Lure Of Politics

If being a World Cultures teacher sparked part of my drive to sponsor Than, additional duties at Bishop O'Hara High School stimulated other interests and pursuits.

As Moderator of the Student Council, Social Studies Department Chairperson, and Bishop O'Hara's Director of Public Relations, I wanted to broaden my community contacts and open up my classroom to prestigious persons in our area and beyond.

My goal was to make learning quite relevant and real. Thus, it became my practice to invite agency and political leaders to the school. I also sponsored field trips to Washington, the United Nations and other centers of government and culture. I took the seniors through the process of voter registration and arranged mock elections with actual voting machines. My American History classes went to the county courthouse to assist with jury selection and observe trial proceedings. My student council presidents annually participated in the prestigious "Presidential Classroom Program" in the Nation's Capital.

Though these were primarily done for my students' education, they produced several pleasant manifestations for me, as well. The places we went and the people we met opened doors to the Arts, Humanities and Politics. Almost every contact and activity made me ripe and ready for more. I hardly recognized the dynamic potential within me until my students made me see it.

I guess there were several omens in my past of the things that would come, but it is only in hindsight that I can trace the progression.

Since early childhood, my family and friends acknowledged my abilities to lead and they encouraged me to be "top dog" in a variety of settings. As I grew older, though the arenas changed, the intricacies and glamour of high profile, high power roles intensified and I found myself inextricably hooked. Interactions with two Presidents and other prominent politicians, school elections and politics, my academic training and the courses I taught sparked my enthusiasm even further.

Such endeavors kept me abreast of contemporary issues and I got increasingly involved in them. I believed in the political process as a means of shaping our world, so finding the right ideology was important to me.

My liberal leanings shifted with age, but I was more an Independent than a Democrat or a Republican. Most of my family had been lifelong "D's". Dad had gotten a job through Republican friends so that was how I registered.

Dad encouraged me to get involved with the city, county and state organizations. At first, much of what I did was low-keyed but in 1975, the incumbent county commissioners wanted more. They asked me to research, analyze and evaluate their first term in office and develop their reelection platform.

Being an integral part of the brainstorming and strategizing proved very exciting. It was fertile ground to test my skills.

In a surprisingly short while, I was writing and making speeches for the team and directing many of the media blitzes. When the commissioners were resoundingly re-elected, all the exposure had pleasant repercussions. They appointed me to the Cultural Affairs and Drug and Alcohol Commissions.

Younger than most of the appointees, I found many seasoned mentors to guide and encourage me.

Chief among them was Brigadier General John McDonald, whom I affectionately nicknamed my "Think Tank". The elder statesman and I became instant friends and I trusted him completely. John groomed and polished me and helped me develop a confident professionalism and a methodical, goal-directed style.

Whether it was he or my students or *Rocky* (the movie), I soon was inspired to directly explore other dimensions of leadership and to toss my hat into the political ring. *Rocky* opened in Scranton as "just another fight movie" that I barely wanted to see, but as I sat in the dark theater watching the underdog beat his odds, personal flashbacks jolted me. The message was a knockout. Rocky Marciano spoke again to me through the character of Rocky Balboa. Each in their own way challenged me to be all I could be and now I truly felt up to that challenge.

The very next day I called John about my intentions. "General, I want to run for office."

I already knew how he would respond.

"Go for it, my boy. I'm with you all the way," he answered exuberantly.

Inspired and excited, I presented my plan to my parents and a few good friends.

"Are you ready for this?" my mother cautioned. "It will take your time and energy."

"He's up to it," my father encouraged.

"What office?" my friend, Charlie wanted to know.

"Borough Tax Collector," I responded, adding, "My accounting degree has prepped me for that."

No one wanted to put a damper on my naively optimistic designs, though several understood the downside of my choice. I had taken on the most powerful figure in the town, the titular head of his party, their top vote getter and I hardly understood the magnitude of my goal.

My opponent had powerful connections and the experience of his incumbency. He was vice-president of the town's biggest bank and as a Democrat, he enjoyed the 9-to-1 registration advantage of his majority party.

But what did I know about any of this? Absolutely nothing. My knowledge was basically from textbooks and I understood far more about national and state governments than anything at the local level and Dunmore was a very political town.

Since the forces entrenched to defeat me were merely incalculable abstractions, my ignorance made it easy to fantasize a win and my optimism and energy were infectious.

My small campaign team and I breezed through the May Primary with no opposition. We thought of ourselves as "Winners" from the start and I hardly ever entertained the possibilities of defeat in November.

Throughout that summer, my support built. We had fun with backyard rallies and fundraisers. I met a lot of people and most of them seemed willing to back me. When the campaign moved to a more visible stage, several of our stalwarts backed off.

General John pinpointed the problem. "Obviously they're afraid the 'political machine' will hurt them. This town operates on the 'Who you know' principle of control and indebtedness and sometimes job security is tied to who you'll support. In that regard your opponent has the upper hand."

John was right. Members of my own family felt the pressure to flee to the other side and I gradually began to see and face the discouraging odds.

I had dealt with bad odds before and simply worked harder and with more determination . . . like a super "Rocky", the combo of Rocky Marciano and Rocky Balboa.

Election Day had our adrenaline pumping. Friends manned every polling station in the borough from 7 a.m. to closing and they gathered at my house to compile the totals. The results from the first three districts saw me behind by small margins. To me, that was a harbinger of defeat. But, my friend Mike thought otherwise.

"If George only has you by twenty to thirty votes in those precincts, you'll kill him in the second and sixth wards."

That made little sense to me, but when those numbers came in, I was ahead by enough votes to make it count. The house erupted with joy. V-I-C-T-O-R-Y was in the air and Charlie screamed, Mike cried, my "team" toasted and a frenzied celebration began in earnest.

Though the hour was late, well-wishers gathered one after another and by 10:30, our house was bursting with over 300 euphoric revelers. My opponent called to concede and wish me well and the media arrived for live coverage at 11:00. They headlined my win as "the greatest political upset in Lackawanna County in over a decade."

Almost too stunned for words, like a scene right out of Robert

Redford's movie *The Candidate*, I looked into the tear-stained face of my friend and campaign coordinator and said, "Charlie, now what do we do?"

We both laughed and Charlie gave out another PRIMAL SCREAM, a fitting symbol of the day - an encouraging blend of the past's perseverance and hard work, the present's impressive success and optimistic indicators for the future.

I felt quite lucky and grateful for my good fortune, confidant that upcoming storms would be weathered the same way - with the love, support and assistance of many caring "significant others". Little did I know how prophetic that feeling would be because waiting in the wings was the wonderful woman, who would usher in the next era of my dreams.

That is the next chapter.

CHAPTER 17

The Love Of My Life

(Mary, sweet Mary, you have entered my life and now I can share the special magic you have given me.)

No one, not even my Grandpa, ever suggested that I would meet the girl of my dreams, woo and court her, make her my bride and link to a loving soul mate, who would love and cherish me for the rest of our lives. By the time, I was thirty; I basically accepted the romantic void and substituted anything I could for tender fulfillment.

Family and friends helped a lot. They generously offered love and sentimentality to many of my experiences and I let fantasies cover the rest. I missed the real thing and secretly longed for a time, a place, and a girl to share my life.

When I read of Romeo and Juliet and the other great romances, I felt cheated. When I witnessed friends and family entwined with their mates, I felt denied. Every wedding underscored my "solitary confinement" and it hurt a lot, but I realized that I had to hedge against the frustration and come to terms with it or allow it to overwhelm me.

It was Franklin Delano Roosevelt who advised, "People in wheelchairs must reconcile themselves to their isolation or suffer additional misery." Surely, he spoke from experience, but he had Eleanor and I had no one.

Over the years, many fine people entered my life and enhanced it with their affections, but all too often, they exited to destinations where I could not follow. It was my fate to sit helplessly back as they followed their dreams and destinies among other people or in other places.

Each separation and parting stung and as I grew older, the pain of every departure and every loss got worse. I coped by clinging steadfastly to what I could. Possessively, I guarded and nurtured those whom I treasured; obsessed with the fears that others might claim them. In my fixations, I knew bad consequences were likely to follow.

When my Grandfather died, at my lowest point, I revealed my possessive love to my Cousin Annie. "I can't give him up - not even to God," I sobbed.

Annie tenderly offered me an explanation and a warning. "You're typical of someone born under the Sign of Cancer. The Crab will give up its claw before it will relinquish its holdings. You just can't and won't let go. Billy, don't be selfish about separation. Don't lose your claw."

I didn't want to be selfish. It hardly fit my image. Annie may have been right. Though I was willing to give of myself and my material possessions, those whom I loved were exclusively mine. I was insanely jealous when Mom and Dad fostered Julia and I resented my grandparents' attention to the other "kids". It even set poorly when my friends gravitated toward new friendships. Having someone and then letting go was a conflict I rarely handled well. Whenever it happened, I tried to be numb and dumb but my obsession would not allow such an easy out. No matter how hard I tried, I was unable to say a graceful "good-bye." Whether the separation was through life or death, I clung to the missing person, physically, mentally and spiritually reluctant to back away.

Knowing of this overpowering trait, I convinced myself that a girlfriend, a lover, a wife would program me for disaster. Maybe it was best that my past flirtations, glamorized infatuations and even the dangerous liaisons lacked any depth, that their scope and scale never amounted too much. I abandoned the quest for the girl of my dreams.

Then along came Mary!

You Can If You Think You Can

Mary was my Cousin Dorothy's close friend. In the summer of 1977, we met at a family picnic and shared a few minutes of light conversation. She offered her assistance for my political campaign and worked with Dorothy on several committees. Then, on the night of my election victory, she showed up to congratulate me, carrying a rose. She kissed me gently on the lips, but others did too. Yet hers was different and the chemistry could not be denied.

I thought about Mary a lot the next day - with mixed feelings of fright and delight. What was going on here? I wondered, half trying to dismiss it.

Thoughts of Mary would not go away and the next time I saw her was at my victory party. There was another rose and another kiss and an added tingle.

Debating no longer, I telephoned her the next day and asked if she might like to stop by for a Thanksgiving Day visit. Her answer was an enthusiastic, "Yes."

My family welcomed her with detached courtesy, but she and I found conversation smooth and easy. The time simply flew and when she left, we agreed to "do it again sometime".

I kept the matter vague so that either of us could re-think our position or gracefully bow out. Mary soon followed through with a time and place, an arrangement just with me "alone".

A-L-O-N-E?

That was the operative word and it rattled my senses. Now the ball was in my camp. Sheepishly, I suggested dinner at the Mai King Restaurant the following Friday and that was perfectly acceptable to her.

During the endless week, I could hardly focus on anything else. I wanted to put my best foot forward, but almost didn't know how. An internal force kept nagging so I had to get it right.

What should I wear? I wondered.

How should I act?

What should I say?

I felt the need to orchestrate every moment but there was something undeniably spontaneous in the making, something beyond my control, so I simply yielded to it. If Cupid decided my moves, that was all right with me.

Yet there were some details I had to arrange and these, as usual, involved a "third party", my dad. It was awkward for both of us, but my father agreed to drive me to my date. I had him stop for a flower, before we picked Mary up, and he brought us to the restaurant and took us to our table. I asked him to return for us around ten.

Finally alone, we captured four hours - to dine, discuss and declare. . so much . . so little. Time flew as we shared our interests and carefully skirted our expectations and everything about the night unfolded much easier than its cumbersome beginnings.

This girl was special and I liked her - a lot. Neither of us was happy to see Dad arrive ten minutes early. The coach turned back into a pumpkin and it wasn't even midnight.

In the days that followed, the phone became our connecting link and Mary and I talked about and around everything, carefully avoiding the intimate "us". That was the agenda for our next date.

Returning to the Mai King, this time I asked Dad to return for us at eleven. With one more hour, it was hardly enough to go from a casual "hello" to the deepest, darkest recesses of our souls, but we both wanted and needed full disclosure.

"If we're going to go anywhere with this, Mary," I began, "it's got to be up front and honest. There are things you need to know."

Then, like the opening of floodgates, many of the thoughts and feelings, that I refused to admit to anyone, myself included, poured out. With brutal force and precision, I cut through all the layers of my complexity and a whole different phase of personal discovery came forth - both for her and me.

The ghosts of hidden fears were not as ominous as I thought and Mary accepted every word, unshocked and empathetic.

"I have my own complications, too," she commented, "and I want to share them with you as well. I appreciate and admire your honesty. It sets me free."

By evening's end, no subject remained taboo. We spit out our concerns, and in that short span, we came to know each other more than many people might in an entire lifetime. We presented ourselves exactly as we were and with blatant honesty; we defined the "us".

From there, there was no place to go but up, and the pace was dizzying. By New Year's Eve, we were ready to launch 1978 as a couple, committed to each other for better or worse. Saying "I love you" validated the surging bond we felt and that thrust us recklessly forward.

Mary and I spoke with each other daily and spent two or three nights together each week - occasionally for dinner or a movie, but usually just for some talk.

In February, Mary's cousin was being invested as Archbishop of Hawaii and her family planned a trip for the ceremonies.

I was excited for her and said so. "It will be spectacular," I noted.

But, obviously, this was not what she wanted to hear.

"I don't want to go," she said, "and I don't want you to want me to go either."

That sounded strange to me and I sat dumbfounded. Her next words startled me even more.

"I want to marry you, Billy," she said.

I was speechless - and unready. "I can't," I said. "It's too much, too soon. You MUST go to Hawaii. We've got to test this thing out."

She rebuffed me. "I'm a mature, responsible woman," she argued. "I know what I need and want."

A tear came to my eye. "But I don't. I need time."

It was an admission that shook my confidence and stopped me in my tracks.

"Mary, I never thought seriously about such things. Being your boyfriend is both my joy and my honor, but being your husband...a week apart might be healthy for both of us."

"We're right for each other, Billy. I know that, and I think you do, too. Take the week if you need it, but listen to your heart."

She spoke tenderly, convincingly and I appreciated the week to re-evaluate what was happening. It was a good time to be alone, and though I missed Mary a lot, my mind needed to clear. Weighing the issues, I realized that Mary gave me a wholeness I never knew existed and I felt truly blessed, but there was a great deal to sort out before I could feel comfortable with the next step.

When Mary returned from Hawaii, we picked up where we had left off and we blended our ideas and interests as our romance blossomed. But finding time to be alone certainly wasn't easy. Her second-floor apartment was inaccessible to me and as a public figure, no dark corner in any restaurant or bar was ever private enough. Since I lived at home with my parents, the most we could manage were a few hours by ourselves in an otherwise unoccupied room. It was a strange way to execute a courtship, but I was accustomed to unusual means to achieve my desired ends -- in that body and my being. Gradually, very gradually, she literally took control of the driver's seat. She had the strength to put me in and out of my adapted Checker Cab and we took rides to distant places. Despite the misgivings and disapproval of my parents, the adjustment was intensely more difficult for Mary. We knew that the only real privacy we might acquire was tied to another place and the opportunity for her to assume more direct hands-on care of me.

It grew more obvious, that their protective style was at odds with the direction that we had hoped to take, and I failed to catch early warning signs that resentments were beginning to build. From my naive perspective, I wanted to believe that everything was copasetic, that Mary and I would carve a life of our own and that my parents would cooperate with the evolution.

I could be content with this, not really enamored with the notion of a marriage. Mary, on the other hand, wanted nothing less. Though she mentioned the option often, it continued to frighten me and I used every technique that I could think of to put her off. My arguments emerged from several viewpoints.

"I've never seen myself as a husband and because marriage really doesn't add to the happiness of its partners. I've witnessed many loving couples commit to a life together only to drag each other down. Mary, we have a good thing going. Why risk it?" I contended. "And what about the physical logistics? I've heard my mother say many times, 'No kitchen is big enough for two women.' She'd probably make you her rival and I certainly don't need that. My father did that to Greg, Than and any other usurper of his Kingdom. I don't want you to become just another unwanted houseguest."

Such defenses put the blame on others, but maybe my biggest obstacle was an encroachment on my limited space. In my lifetime, so few of my personal choices and freedoms occurred without the watchful (though caring) eyes of a second party, that my bed represented my only exclusive domain. Wouldn't marriage claim that too?

You Can If You Think You Can

When I presented my rationalizations to Mary, she countered with her own strong refute. Point by point she wisely strengthened a foundation for what she was sure would come. She rented an accessible apartment, where we could play at being a marriage-in-the works, and seeing her in her own environment was important to me.

Mary was a marvel. She could cook, clean and organize a comfortable household, even while managing her professional career as an Educational Diagnostician. Surely she was more than worthy of any man and I was lucky that she had selected me to be by her side.

Yet, despite all that, bachelorhood still seemed better or at least less complex than being a married man. Thus we were at an impasse, and both of us hoped that fate would resolve the troublesome conflict, which dampened the bliss of our otherwise happy state. I tried to emphasize the moment and shy away from the prospects of what might be ahead. Days passed into weeks, into months, into years.

By Christmas of 1982, after five years of courtship, I presented her with a diamond. To me it symbolized the love, trust and bond we shared; to her it meant much more. As she proudly displayed it to family and friends, the stock response was, "Have you set a date?"

"A date? A date for what?" I wondered.

Unschooled in courting etiquette, I had no idea of what I had done. The ring altered Mary's status . . in her own mind and the minds of my parents. They drifted into separate enemy camps.

From that day forward, tensions accompanied almost everything we did together and I was the pivotal point, saddled with the great compromises to make things work.

That compelled me to sacrifice anything I may have desired for a harmony among the rest. It forced compensation after compensation and I felt like I was losing my personal identity once again

If not for other successes, I might have slumped to an unmanageable low. It was the time of other recognitions and they uplifted my spirit. The Scranton Jaycees named me "Teacher of the Year" and Phi Delta Kappa concurred making me their "Educator of the Year". I won the United Nations Peace Award and my second profession in politics was on the ascendancy too.

With the completion of a full term as Borough Tax Collector, the

Republican Party and my supporters wanted me to seek a bigger office -- the Lackawanna County Clerk of Judicial Records position. The size and scope of this undertaking were ten times broader than my first election, but the challenge had its own energy and appeal. Dunmore knew and respected me from my childhood, but would a vaster arena be similarly inclined? The answer was a resounding "yes" and my life shifted dramatically to another stage. Suddenly, I was out of Dunmore and teaching, and thrust into the courthouse with the most powerful and prestigious leaders of the community as my peers.

My ego inflated and I half-believed that I was fulfilling a messianic destiny for which I had been born. I toyed with the mental image of Cecil B. DeMille sitting next to God melodramatically directing me toward achievements of grandeur and glory. A Moses of Modern Times. King William in a Camelot of today

Though I understood that no one was meant to have it all, in the grand scheme of things my lot was good enough for me. If only others could be equally content.

CHAPTER 18

Changes And Challenges

Control has been a big issue with me I guess I'm happiest when I am running the show. Dependency minimizes control and I often found my limitations discouraging and distasteful.

For the most part, I came to accept certain aspects of my subservience early on. I learned to weather many storms, even some of hurricane proportions but there always seemed to be another squall waiting over the horizon. I longed for quiet ports in the storms to recharge for the next major gale.

When my household stabilized for peaceful coexistence and my career brought me prominence and security, I thought I had finally captured the Good Times. I basked in the glories of being my own boss, ruling the roost and having it my way.

Content with all that, Muscular Dystrophy mattered less. I had overcome my ridiculous body's powerlessness and snared the brass ring. Though turbulent waters had calmed, more serious problems were brewing yet again.

It seems the cycle of ebb and flow proves never-ending. Just when I thought I could nestle in and enjoy my loved ones and my life, our family came under attack again. Cancer returned to besiege us.

Much to my surprise, my dad followed the prescribed course for his recovery, admirably accepting his colonostomy and its multiple humiliations. I guess he was just grateful to have survived. Cancer refused to leave my father alone. It recurred again this time in his liver and this occurrence was even more complex than the first.

"We can't treat you here," his specialist told him. "You'll need to go to New York's Sloan Kettering for treatment."

With no other options, Dad went to Manhattan for a six-week process. That placed a great strain on our family. Mom was torn between my needs and his and we were forced to devise a workable course of action.

With Mary's help and that of General John and my friends Mike and Jerry, Mom took daily trips into the city. There she sat vigil beside Dad for eight hours before someone brought her back home. Mary and three of my cousins took over my primary care and every Saturday or Sunday we visited Dad, too.

Everyone cooperated wholeheartedly to address the family crisis as we stretched to the limit. I anguished for my parents and marveled at their mutual love and commitment and I knew that Mary's love and dedication to me were every bit as great.

Our symbiotic abilities to manage these demanding days made me confident that, when Dad came home, things would be better than ever. As wounded beasts all, we helped in each other's healing, so, for the moment, the savagery to control subsided. No one was all-powerful here and we peacefully accepted that. Our vulnerabilities had leveled the playing field for Dad's return.

As Dad recovered and grew stronger, his fight for life became another issue of control. It was as if his survival had empowered him to reclaim and govern us, to micro-manage me in every way.

For me, those hurdles had been successfully jumped, but it was back once again to square one. This time, though, it was worse. Because we had come so close to losing him, I gave in to Dad's patriarchal pronouncements. I returned to the role of his baby.

With every "You can't do this" or "You mustn't do that" I felt my resentments building. I hated what he was doing to me, but I wasn't the only one being victimized by my father's restored forcefulness. Mary, too, felt his stings and she saw her hopes of marriage slipping away even further. Tenaciously she fought back with matching venom.

You Can If You Think You Can

Poor Mom played referee. This was not *Rocky*; it was *The Rocky Horror Picture Show.*

I doubt that any of us wanted it this way, but a destructive flame torched the very dearest people in my life, and I prayed for an end to my misery.

Quite despondent about these conflicts and emotions, I grew unexpressive. My glum silence turned a "cold shoulder" to the offending parties, who were already hurting enough.

Certainly, my antisocial style proved futile and unproductive, and I knew it, but I persisted in my methods. That deepened my depression and Mary, Dad and Mom often asked what was "bugging" me.

At my wits end, I finally blurted out, "You are bugging me. You're tearing me apart. I don't want us to continue these tensions. Your hidden agendas are making enemies of us all. This has got to stop or I don't know what I'll do."

Indeed there was a violent threat in my tone and my implication.

Because Dad, Mom and Mary collectively pleaded ignorance to the causes of my despair, I became much more explicit.

"You each have your own desires. Your damn unwillingness to compromise puts me smack in the middle. Well, I'm no referee for your every word and action. Let's discuss this, openly and honestly, no holds barred."

I went on, "I'll give you three days. You'd better think about how we're going to get through this life TOGETHER. Think it from our gut and be prepared to say it all. If you need to, get someone to support you. That might keep us all civil and sane."

I knew my ultimatum was risky, but I felt it had to be done.

As per my request and timetable, eight anxious people assembled in our living room to confront our ghosts. General John McDonald advocated for me. Mom and Dad had their cousins, Betty and Joe Caputo. Mary asked Harlene Arenberg, her respected confidant, to be by her side.

We had the team we trusted, but the tension was obvious from the start. Over the next two hours, we cried, laughed, and bared our souls. By God's good graces and a collective wisdom, we somehow got through it and came to a workable understanding of each other. Equally important, we formed a pact to face each other and live out some respectful compromises, day by day.

Though Mary and Dad clung to some mutual resentments, they agreed to advance our collective relationships to the next logical phase. I was glad to finally get the matter behind me, behind us, because other things were calling for my attention.

Ever since I was a child, I had been summoned many times to take up the cause of the disabled, but I gracefully sidestepped that mission. Though I tried to mask it, I was uncomfortable in the presence of handicapped people. I really didn't want to identify with them or welcome them actively into my life. They showed me too many things about myself that I really preferred not to face. There was a persistent knocking at my door and every pounding got louder.

At Bishop O'Hara, the administration saw the logic of placing "special needs" students in my classes. Certainly, I never minded that level of exposure. In fact, students with limitations brought out my skills as an educator and I derived a great deal of personal satisfaction from guiding them along. It took me back to my own high school days, when my teen peers taught me many interesting lessons of life.

O'Hara was a model for mainstreaming and maybe my presence was a catalyst for the integration of handicapped youngsters. As I worked with them in a classroom setting, I learned many things, too. I noticed that personality played a huge role in social acceptance, that more hung-up or introverted students had greater difficulties. That partially explains why Anne, a blind girl, may have been the brightest in her class but her aloof nature set her apart. Yet outgoing, handsome, deaf Tony became a football hero and "Most Popular Boy". Obviously, disability was only one of many factors that impact on happiness and success.

Timing is certainly another. I had some students, who were disabled from birth, and others, who came by their disabilities later in life. Renee and Martha never knew what it was like to have a healthy body. Their adjustments, adaptations, compensations were skills they honed through many years. Mike and Donna, on the other hand, had accidents and illnesses that changed them in an instant.

Such contrasts and comparisons illuminated those insights which made me a better, more understanding teacher. By observing the actions and reactions of the able-bodied or able-minded to those who were thought of as "different", I got a handle on how we all might fit together.

Sharing that with my students made me really feel good. Dealing with adults who had impairments was a different story. Personable, friendly, extroverted me found it uncomfortable to socialize among them and I avoided such encounters. Though I felt guilty about it, I wanted no part of their world.

I was not to be let alone. Three distinct groups came beckoning persistently, each with a different purpose.

Very Special People (VSP) wanted me in their spiritual worship. Operation Overcome (OO) had practical civil and political issues for me to tackle and the Deutsch Institute wanted me to enhance the cultural and social life of their organization. Just causes, all.

Did they really need me? I argued to their leaders.

"Yes." "Yes!" "YES!!" they proclaimed and refused to see it any other way.

"You owe it to us," said Earl Ransom of OO. "You're the lucky one who made it. Don't let us down. If you don't help us, we'll only crawl."

His forceful mandate haunted me. The words rang of truth, but his look of desperation sealed the deal.

Faster than I might have ever imagined, I was sucked into the vortex, hurled to its energetic core. The most economically deprived, undereducated, underserved, devalued, degraded, disregarded minority in the nation was screaming at me.

"We are shut in and shut out. In the survival of the fittest, we are the most endangered species. Help us to survive. Give us a voice. Unite us. A movement without movement is no movement at all."

I heard them and understood their plea. It was time to give in. But what was my mission? How, when and where might I achieve it? The questions were difficult; the answers, even more so. But I was in it for the duration. With such vital needs at stake, I had to define the problem and the players and strategies for each.

I was in a rather unique niche, a severely disabled person born and raised in "the mainstream". That meant I saw the issues from many sides. The "many sides" were usually at odds. Thus building linkages, finding strength and support, awareness and understanding from several camps was a logistical nightmare.

History had built gargantuan barriers between all such groups and a biased society was ill prepared for a budding revolution. Able-bodied people emerged from two basic schools: let's help and include or let's ignore and shut out.

The able -- at least most of them -- had the purest of intentions. Helping sometimes actually meant not helping. It only perpetuated the pathetic image of a "collective abomination, a drain on resources, a useless, parasitic lump of crippled misfits who weren't worth the room they took up." That perception hamstrung the potential for real growth and self-actualization.

On the other hand, persons with disabilities tended to be either militant or wimps. The armed warriors resented "the do-gooders", who felt satisfied by lending a helping hand to the "misfits and unfortunates". They saw such people as a part of the enemy along with the wimpy disabled, who humbly and gratefully accepted the handouts. It was their belief that discrimination and prejudice were often cushioned in charitable, humane tokenism assuaged by telethons and drives. They wanted a "real commitment" to equal rights.

Bringing such people together, when they hardly agreed to acknowledge each other, could only occur through education. My remedies came from solid information and a dialogue for solutions. So, I wrote for and spoke to groups, large and small. At local, state and national levels, I discovered many willing ears and eyes that responded to my messages.

The momentum and credibility built as significant steps were taken to alter the status quo, but the demands on my time, energies and abilities mounted, and other personal interests got pushed aside. My identity was changing again.

Being and setting the example compelled me to be more open than ever. I was the "PUBLIC PERSON"; the El Cid of the disabled, called upon by many to address quests for justice and right.

With proper support, I sparked the innovative vanguard for accessibility, attendant care, independent living, least restrictive education, supported employment, nondiscrimination and the legislation to press them into realities.

Surely, internal satisfaction and public recognition rewarded my efforts. I was honored with several prestigious accolades (National Human Services Volunteer, Disabled Wall of Fame, Pennsylvanian of the Year and others) and the ceremonial presentations filled Mary and my parents with joyous pride.

They deserved that because their sacrifices and commitments were every bit as great as mine. We traveled together to many places (Harrisburg, Washington, wherever the need beckoned) and life "on the road" really broadened my insights and perspectives. In the many colorful associations, I got opportunities to stretch and flex my creative muscles.

Imagination and resourcefulness served me well as the design for social changes found concrete expression. Gradually programs emerged which advanced the survival and quality of life for the handicapped. Literally millions benefited from such measures as The National Rehabilitation Act and Public Law 94-142, equal education in the least restrictive environment.

It was most gratifying to see the alterations and progress that spelled improved opportunities for those who would have been otherwise denied. That added to my sense of purpose and worth. Such fulfillment built an even healthier base for me to manage my own issues.

Yet, the challenge to not get lost in the "Big Picture" became a delicate balancing act. It demanded a careful monitoring so that my priorities would be kept straight and I would remain true to myself. That wasn't easy when ego interfered.

So how do you manage that?

CHAPTER 19

The Loss

The scope of changing commitments dramatically altered my life. My arena of neighborhood, family, friends, Dunmore, Scranton, Pennsylvania gave way to new places and associations. I became a traveler with the adventuresome compulsions of Columbus. However, on land, on sea or in the air, locations never before seen presented many unexpected obstacles.

When I was a child, my lighter, stronger, more balanced body could be transported in ordinary cars, cabs and busses. As the wheelchair entered my life and my upper body weakened, the demand for alternative, adapted vehicles was mother to invention.

In 1952, Dad converted our new car, a Nash Rambler, by removing the front passenger seat. Engineers arranged space for my wheelchair and we may have had the nation's first adapted passenger car. Over the years, we similarly retrofitted a couple of Checker cabs before giving in to a factory-built HP van.

As I matured to driving age, counselors pressed me to graduate from passenger to driver with hand-operated controls, but I had no real success with a motorized wheelchair, and I had no desire to navigate anything bigger.

There were a host of other difficulties centering on physical accessibility beyond just a car. Well-intentioned friends often sent me to places, where rugged terrain and steep stairways shut me out. Many doorways, rest rooms, hotel and motel rooms and the like were ill-equipped to accommodate me. Sometimes, my bladder seemed ready to explode, before we could locate a bathroom, where nature could take its course. In New York City, stops at the Hilton were necessary since it had the only Men's Room I was able to use.

Yet, my role as an advocate for the disabled and my own personal desires made public transportation and reasonable access quite significant issues. In the 1960s and 1970s, there was little to guide or direct me. I had to be a pioneer. The risks were great, but duty and wanderlust compelled me to explore and enjoy. If I REALLY wanted to see Disney world, and I did, I had to fly.

The trip to Orlando would take me 1200 miles from home. Because our small, local airport had no jet way, and I did not want to be carried up the steps, we needed to depart from the Philadelphia airport. Unfortunately, our car broke down on the way. During the rush hour, we were twenty miles short of the terminal.

"What can we do?" my mother asked in dismay.

My uncle suggested, "Why don't we contact the State Police to assist us?"

After a phone call, a policeman soon arrived to lend us a hand. He jumped to several wrong conclusions, assuming a medical emergency as the reason for our flight. He summoned an ambulance and an eight-car escort whisked us across the fast moving lanes of the Skulykill Expressway. The ambulance, with lights flashing and sirens blazing, made its way to the airport in a hurry.

When it became obvious that we would still be late, someone radioed ahead to hold the plane. After the frenzy of the motorcade, we finally arrived but the 737 had taxied to the end of the runway. By-passing all the metal detectors and baggage handlers, I was carried up the steps, right into "First Class". The crew bent over backwards to expedite things further, but in their haste, they bent the frame of my wheelchair too. It wickedly pulled to the left ever after. We loved Mickey Mouse anyway.

Since tackling the friendly sky was an amazing achievement, it was now time to sail onward - to the sea.

A cruise was Mom's lifetime dream vacation and she had saved for it for years. The fund built and the whole family (my parents, Grandma, Mary, and I) prepared to go off to the islands. Barbara, our travel agent, called the Homeric Line for arrangements. With us by her side, she carefully and competently spelled out all our special needs, including the dimensions of the wheelchair. The line assured us that the staterooms would be large enough, but they noted that some of the ports-of-call might be inaccessible.

"That's good enough for me," Mom consented. So, we committed to the cruise.

As a convenience and for safety, the crew boarded me first. We soon discovered that the door to our stateroom was too narrow. After several unworkable options, a steward vice-gripped the frame of my chair to fit the doorway. It uncomfortably squeezed me all week. But even worse, I was a "prisoner" on the ship at every disembarkation. No harbor was accessible.

Needless to say, the multiple difficulties and disappointments made for a pretty miserable trip. We collectively vowed that this would be our first AND last cruise.

Such awful experiences led me to co-found the National Travel Task Force For People With Disabilities. In that role, I was commissioned to ride Amtrak from Harrisburg to Philadelphia to Washington, D. C. to evaluate and videotape their stations and trains. They scheduled me on accessible cars.

From the very first lap of the journey, arrangements fell apart and I jiggled about in the unheated, metal antechamber at the car's entrance for two hours. Unable to see anything, alone and blasted by the unmuffled clanging of the iron rails, I finally arrived in Philly, totally wiped out. Although the next lap to D. C. was not as bad, various changes and delays cost me over $500 in added expenses.

This was a small part of the price I paid as a volunteer advocate, but things needed to be fixed, (back door or through-the-kitchen pathways to luxury places, inferior, or no-option seating in theaters, restaurants and churches and countless second-class-citizen treatments). I vowed to help.

The snowballing momentum to do just that was undeniable and "the movement" grew in size, scope and significance. With the passage of the 1964 Civil Rights Act, then the National Rehabilitation Act, the Architectural Barrier Removal Law and other measures, a new day had dawned. The shut-out and shut-in emerged from their hovels to be counted.

Politically, socially, culturally, economically, they (we) were free at last.

This was an ongoing and ever-changing process. Like a complex Chess Game, much was at stake and I was in the dead center of it all. The very changes impacting on the masses were changing me too.

With Mary's perspective, encouragement and support, I felt empowered to actualize my rights; rights I once never knew I had. Accepting my own strength to assert myself, this pussycat became a tiger. As my hang-ups and vulnerabilities gave way to brutal, honest, comfortable self-expression, I felt primed for almost anything.

There is always that unexpected surprise.

At the time when global, exterior causes were beckoning and I was enthusiastically responding, crisis was taking hold again, right under my roof.

Dad's cancer was back and the battle to survive started anew. We thought he had licked it - twice. For a few years, he appeared to be doing just fine. He worked by my side, as my administrative assistant, and we managed to make the proximity tolerable.

There were the usual clashes and challenges, but I finally had an adult identity in my father's mind. He was very proud of what I had become and he eased up on orchestrating my life. Yet, the duty and dedication to serve and protect me remained intact. Reluctantly, more gracefully, he accepted the care from others. He knew he was dying.

We kept on seeking his cure, but every attempt proved lame and futile. Chemotherapy brought him one step forward and two steps back. He suffered a lot, physically, mentally, emotionally and we witnessed his daily torment and torture and obvious decline. He kept fighting for my sake and Mom's.

We traveled to the Georgetown Medical Center, where a transplant was suggested as a possible hope, but tests showed the cancer was too widespread and he was rejected. Our silent collective despair accompanied the eerie homecoming.

It was a re-election year, 1989, and Dad's health was a significant factor. A lot still had to be done and maybe that was a blessing in disguise. It offered some distractions.

Dad attempted to make the rounds with me as I pranced about to meet and greet the electorate. Often he grimaced and gritted his teeth, as he valiantly tried to muster enough strength to maintain the grueling pace. It became a tough call to encourage or discourage his participation. He was there, when and how he could be.

The extra pressure of his health and Mom's emotional condition made this campaign altogether different. If it were not for Mary and my always-zealous army (the General, Charlie, Mike, Tom, Bill, Paul, Joe and the others), I might have packed it in, but they picked up the slack and kept me energized. Though I never doubted the election's outcome, a heavy heart overshadowed this victory.

Yet, something else created cause for joy . . my marriage to Mary.

Wedding plans have a unique power to uplift the spirit and we wanted our union to be a fitting celebration tailor-made, to capture the twelve years we had already shared, for better or worse, in sickness and in health.

The ingredients were carefully selected to make this the most important day of our lives. It was our gift to each other, as well as to the good families and friends, who would join us that day. Who better to be my Best Man than my dad? Again, he was at my side, giving me to Mary and the world, yet clinging a little bit until . .

Six months later, he was ready to really let go.

From the day of our wedding, Dad had a steadier, quicker decline. I saw this powerful man whither before me and the angel nurses of Hospice, Nancy and Diane, guided us through the process of his wind-down, supporting us throughout.

It was an unexpectedly peaceful time. We felt the healthiest bond of mutual love and understanding that we had ever known.

In the final days, Nancy told my mom and me, "He must hear and know that you have given him permission to go." I was on the back porch as the receiver monitor made me a reluctant eavesdropper to my parents' last good-byes. How truly beautiful was their love! That night I found the courage to say good-bye, too.

On July 25, 1990, Dad slipped into a coma and the Hospice nurses sat vigil with Mom in the last few hours.

On the morning of July 25, 1990, my Cousin Don awakened me very early. "Your father needs you," he said.

He helped me get to my father's bedside. Dad's chest was undulating through shallow labored breaths. I took his right hand in mine. "I'm here," I said.

Dad smiled contentedly. His breathing eased. Then he died. His body gave up its fight but his spirit soared triumphantly.

The next day President Bush signed the Americans With Disabilities Act, our nation's most comprehensive Civil Rights legislation in history. How fitting! I can picture my dad smiling proudly and confidently as he sits next to God and Cecil B. DeMille as the epic continues.

CHAPTER 20

Deal With It And Move On.

Epics tell dramatic sagas of great heroes embarking on a quest for their dreams, desires, destinations and destinies. Their struggles involve positive and negative forces, dastardly villains and unexpected twists. Yet, the central character plods along. In the trials and tribulations that our hero encounters, some universal truth is finally understood.

The "quest" is part of everyone's story, a common thread linking us as one. Despite our separations and differences, the challenges, which prod, poke and provoke us, teach us the lessons of Life. Though there are few "definites", every person and every situation we experience offers an opportunity that undoubtedly defines us.

Looking back over my own fifty-five years, I've attempted to sort out who and what I am. The gut punches probably mattered more than the fluff. In them, came revelation and truth.

When my father died, it was a very tough time. Like the devastating loss of loved ones, who went their way before him, I had very mixed emotions, confusions about the cosmic whys. I felt cheated, denied, detached. Someone had come and gone in body. Yet, something else held fast. There had to be a meaning in this seeming dichotomy and I needed to understand it.

You Can If You Think You Can

I found my answers through another movie. Shortly after my dad's funeral, Mary and I went to see *Ghost*. The film's main character was called Sam, my dad's nickname.

As scene followed scene, I found other startling parallels too. Sam was a protector. His mission was to secure the well-being of his loved one - still communicating, still assisting - from an energy beyond the human form. Death had not changed that mission. If anything, death only enhanced it.

Though *Ghost* was just a film fantasy, it spoke volumes to me. I found comfort in its glorification of the spirit, I understood that Thutaron, Grandpa, Steve, Bob, JFK, Rocky, Dad and so many others transcended Time. They remained connected, inspiring, encouraging and energizing. They were the Force, a part of me forever.

And maybe that is the essence of God.

Such feelings turned pain into peace. Probably more than most, I had witnessed death's parade and its consequences and *Ghost* added another dimension to my awareness. But that centered on the mortality of others. What about my own?

Though MD posed a lingering threat to me, I hardly addressed the nuisance, staying distracted by the joy of life. My focus was on each breathing, active day. Yet an unexpected accident suddenly shifted that focus and brought a pressing challenge to my own survival.

In the fall of 1993, an incident occurred, which sparked another shift in my thinking.

One morning, much like many others, Mom administrated an enema to help me eliminate. Pushing harder than usual, she inadvertently punctured my bowel. I felt the deep penetration and the pain but for one long, hurting week, I concealed my distress. When intermittent fevers rose to 104 degrees and I grew delirious, however, Mary realized something was wrong. Despite my protests, she took me to the hospital.

In minutes, my condition was noted as severe peritonitis.

"You are in pretty serious shape," my doctor acknowledged.

He continued. "We can administer mega doses of antibiotics, but if we cannot control the infection, would you want any extraordinary measures?"

He had made it my call. My choice. How should I answer?

Since quality of life ranked higher with me than quantity, what might these extraordinary measures mean? If that translated into added burdens for Mary and Mom or undignified suffering for me, then why bother?

Yet, the primal struggle for survival persisted within me. I was not ready to die. After seventy-two hours of intensive care and massive amounts of intravenous drugs, my infection was brought under control. The critical period had ended.

I remained in the hospital eleven more days. These were heavy, reflective times and I reviewed my extraordinary life over and over again. There was so much to consider - where I had been and where I needed to go. The soul-searching process set me on a different course, one with far greater respect for the future.

More attentive to limits, I discussed a plan with Mary. We had to re-establish our priorities. Since we wanted to share more experiences together, Mary took her retirement. Now we could pursue our calculated dreams - a family, a business, the development of my writing aspirations and travel.

We grounded our game plan in reality, seeking to manage the obstacles ahead through contentment in each other. If we were satisfied with the simple, then our most basic needs (health, happiness, fulfillment and inner peace) would surely be enough.

But such fine treasures are not easy to come by, even with the best-laid plans. Muscular Dystrophy had never left me and it continued to do its thing. As I lost the remaining strength in my right arm and my other muscles weakened, I could no longer hold a magazine, book, paint brush, playing cards or game pieces. Looking in the mirror, I could not deny the malformed, struggling being fighting to maintain function and dignity. This was a harsh enough reality. Yet, that mirror now reflected even more, an "older" man with the paranoia of a mid-life crisis.

I wanted to believe that MD would have spared me. That it would have made me immune to cancer, heart disease or other life-threatening conditions, but my body told me otherwise. Once I had lived virtually pain free. Now the era of aching bones, bruised tissue and organ impairments was upon me.

I learned by teasing, taunting degrees that forty is different from twenty and thirty and I felt the consequences inside and out, top to toe. My skin began to break down. Pressure sores caused inconveniences and discomfort to my butt and feet. Severe sleep apnea sapped my energies and my own blood gases almost poisoned me. I struggled to bring oxygen to my body and brain through restless nights and exhausting days. My eyes deteriorated so that I could hardly see anything clear enough to enjoy it.

These God-awful problems further limited my already-restricted life and I was discouraged. I often wondered how these new setbacks might impact on my plans and aspirations and that was pretty frightening.

Mary never faltered. She was my strength. She did the homework, and with her support, I faced the rounds of doctors and treatments and adaptations and adjustments. Together, we found ways to regain some functions. Special cushions, altered seating, a CPAP breathing unit and oxygen compressor and Radial Keratotomy restored my "machinery". They reversed the temporary set backs and I, we, zealously resumed the pursuit of our goals.

But with my own health problems resolved, those of our family took their place. Mary and I were the middle-aged children of old, declining, needy parents and relatives. They were our most cherished and respected friends, and we simply could not turn our backs on them. It became our responsibility to assist them through their twilight years, gently orchestrating their care.

One by one, they faced the medical emergencies and complex challenges that required our support and energies. Again, we were pulled in many directions. We owed them whatever we could do and we willingly accepted that commitment. This was untested territory for us. In many ways, we were unprepared for the emotional, mental and physical role-reversals which such a commitment demands. It took many delicate steps to preserve their identities and dignities.

Like them, I had known dependency and could empathize with their feelings and frustrations. Yet, they were once the providers, the caregivers. It was sad to see them give in to us as their mainstays. For them, there was no recovery, only prolonged deterioration and steady decline.

Being witness to their decline made Mary and me long for that important missing link in our lives - children. But was it too late for that?

Mary and I often talked about that void, praying something, someone, could fill it. We carefully weighed the ways to integrate children into the grand constellation. Our ship was already overloaded with needs and that would not be fair to any child, natural or otherwise. Therefore, practicality compelled us to forego that dream.

Our austere, simple design for a better, more manageable life slipped further away. Then, just when things seemed to border on another crisis, Divine Intervention provided a fulfilling solution. That's where Tommy and Rich come in.

Both Tom and Rich were young men, when they entered our lives. Like Greg, they came at a particularly critical time. With their energy and caring, they saw our needs and stood by our side during increasingly burdensome days. Tom and Rich became our saving grace to stay the course and overcome the obstacles.

Tommy and I met through political connections, but in a short while, we opened up a dialogue to broader things. Though I was sixteen years older, he and I shared similar attitudes and values. His honesty and openness built my trust, so I offered him a job in the Clerk's Office.

Tommy's professional potential was apparent from the start. He quickly absorbed everything I could hope to teach him and then some. He was willing, eager and capable of any challenge I presented and I thought of him as my young protégé. During a rather sticky legal battle that erupted at work, Tommy showed tremendous courage. His masterful handling of the problem proved he had the right stuff to merit special status in my life.

Tom has a fine wife, three beautiful sons, an adopted child and intermittent foster children. They have welcomed us warmly as their extended family. Mary and I enjoy their vitality and exuberance. It uplifts us often as the connection continues.

Rich is ten years younger than Tom. He was a junior at the University of Scranton when we met. He answered my ad for a "Personal Care Attendant" posted on a bulletin board.

From the second we met, Rich demonstrated an uncanny sense

of my mental, physical and emotional needs along with a remarkable ability to meet them. His interests and activities brought back happy memories of my past because he was very much like me. Again, I had glimpses of what I might have been if Muscular Dystrophy had not altered my agenda.

Rich was an idealist, a high-minded optimist striving to make this a far better world. I loved watching him tirelessly swim laps in our pool, devour Tom Clancey and John Grisham novels, plan his future and court his own lovely Mary. He stood at the threshold of manhood and I was there to watch him cross over. I am still so very proud of the man he has become.

Thus, Tommy and Rich were like the mirror, reflecting and recalling me at twenty and thirty. Those images placed age in its appropriate setting, unthreatening and purposeful. These vibrant young men counterbalanced the important senior citizens in our every day and that symbiotic harmony created the balance I needed to see. It demonstrates the bond, the valuable link that ties us together, people to people, for soaring collective achievements.

In all this, I discovered that being in the middle was a pretty good place to be. From that perspective, I could look ahead and back and see the overall scheme of things. Maybe for too many years I overemphasized age, dependency and what ifs. Now, I believe that you can never really know. But, so what?

Like the message in *Forrest Gump*, you have to sample the chocolates if you want to experience the taste. Live the illusion. Make the reel real. You can if you think you can.

In my MOVIE, it has been my good fortune to have played many parts: son, husband, relative, neighbor, friend, teacher, administrator, activist, advocate, spokesperson, artist, writer, mentor, traveler, volunteer, dreamer, thinker, philosopher and believer - in me and in humanity.

It is really nice to know that I am a part of an ensemble cast. My successes and my failures are commingled with a whole army of loving, caring foot soldiers, who walk for me and with me, on my journey.

Thus the epic continues.

As I chronicle what has been, I am content with what is and confidant about my future - our future - and the progress and prospects of our species.

I will hold tight to every moment and every being because each is a fabulous part. Together, we validate and perpetuate our existence towards a universal, cosmic wonder that is sure to capture eternity for us all.

I truly believe that from the depths of my heart, mind and soul. Thus, I believe that this is not. . **THE END.**

Epilogue

My Typical Day

At the specific request of Dr. Harold Dawley, the publisher of this book, I am adding a description of a typical day for me.

Muscular Dystrophy, the killing disease attacking my body, has not shut me out nor made me powerless. Though it could have consumed me with fright and frustration, I have developed the tenacity to overcome its insidiousness and establish a positive purpose for my life. I have built personal and professional successes as a respected educator, competent businessman, credible public official, community leader and acknowledged advocate for the Arts, Justice and human rights.

I cherish my life and its challenges have only made me stronger. They pump me up to transcend the limits, revel in the triumphs and activate my urge to tell the world just who I am.

To that end, let me share a "typical day".

My morning begins at seven, when my wife Mary turns off and detaches the CPAP and oxygen machines, that have helped me breathe through the night. After other supports are removed, she and an attendant get me to a sitting position for breakfast. With a small box as a fulcrum, I am able to feed myself, and though I struggle a bit, the extra effort seems worth it. I wish I could be equally self-sufficient for the next tasks, the very private functions of bladder and bowel. I guess I have never fully adjusted to the presence of my compassionate caregivers during this phase of my routine, but I have accepted it nonetheless.

An exhilarating bed bath comes next. Besides sound hygiene, the scrub stimulates blood flow and primes my skin to avoid breakdown. Range of motion and stretching exercises follow, and since they enhance respiration and muscle tone and deter the deformity and contractions common to MD, we are attentive to every repetition. When the physical therapy is completed, Mary and my attendant begin to dress me. My clothes are carefully chosen for unrestricted movement and seams, lines and wrinkles are put in their place to insure my comfort and function.

Finally, after some three hours, I am ready to get out of bed. My attendant positions me in my wheelchair and takes me to the bathroom to brush my teeth, wash and comb my hair, give me a shave and spritz me with cologne. Next, come socks, shoes, shirt, tie and the next set of challenges for my day.

The obstacles outside my home are many and varied. Though I have a special van, inclement weather, road contours, construction, rapid accelerations and heavy braking give me a thrilling ride. With neck muscles too weak to support my head and no upper body strength to hold me in place, any unexpected circumstances can toss or tumble me. Yet accidents, bruises, aches and breaks are far better than home confinement and I am always eager to tackle my professional responsibilities, day by day.

I am the Lackawanna County Clerk of Judicial Records for Lackawanna County, Pennsylvania. My job consists of administering a twenty person staff and overseeing the management of the court related records and documents. The environment has been tailored to suit my skills and automated equipment allows me full control of my work. With speaker phones, computers, printers, and Fax, I have what I need to perform my duties effectively and I take pride in a job well done.

When the workday is over, depending on demands or desires, I may go off to a movie, a meeting, a visit with friends or a romantic dinner with my wife. Then I return home where TV, the VCR and the computer set me free to explore, escape and feel another grand range of enriching possibilities. Thankfully, the benefits of finger-flicking devices offer pleasant substitutes for some of my lost pastimes, so I remain quite content.

After the eleven o'clock news, more therapy, medication, positioning and machine hookups, it is time for bed, dreaming and the happy expectations of tomorrow.

You Can If You Think You Can

Though I cannot deny that Muscular Dystrophy is an annoyance, it has not broken my spirit. Instead it has given me an opportunity to draw upon something special, to shed my hang-ups and to deal with my fears. It has actually made me STRONG - not in body but in mind and spirit. And isn't that what matters most?

Help Is But A Click Away -

A MESSAGE FROM THE PUBLISHER

In my troubled youth, I discovered the hope and knowledge available in self-help books. I subsequently became a psychologist and went on to write five self-help books. I was so impressed by the power of self-help books that when the Internet became so prevalent in our lives, I realized it was the ideal place for people to find help. *SelfHelpBooks.com* emerged and is readily available to anyone who is in need of help.

SelfHelpBooks.com publishes books by mental health professionals as well as by lay people who have coped with life's adversity and have valuable advice to pass on to the rest of us. The titles that can be found in *SelfHelpBooks.com*'s virtual bookstore have been carefully selected to provide help for a range of problems from addiction to depression, from fear to loneliness, and from problems of youth to problems of the elderly.

At *SelfHelpBooks.com* we think we have a book for almost every problem. If you need help immediately, you can download it as an E book. If you are in less of a hurry, you can order a print version and receive it within days.

If you visit SelfHelpBooks.com and don't find a book relating to your particular problem, contact us and we will immediately add books in that category. If you know of a particular self-help book that has helped you, let us know and we will add it to our list as well.

Harold H. Dawley, Jr., Ph.D., ABPP
Publisher

Printed in the United States
756100007B